George Norcross

The story of a thirtieth anniversary. Rev. George Norcross

In the Second Presbyterian Church

George Norcross

The story of a thirtieth anniversary. Rev. George Norcross
In the Second Presbyterian Church

ISBN/EAN: 9783337257309

Printed in Europe, USA, Canada, Australia, Japan

Cover: Foto ©Lupo / pixelio.de

More available books at **www.hansebooks.com**

THE STORY

OF

A THIRTIETH ANNIVERSARY.

REV. GEORGE NORCROSS, D. D.,

IN THE

SECOND PRESBYTERIAN CHURCH,

CARLISLE, PA.

Published by the Board of Trustees.

CARLISLE, PA.:
HERALD STEAM PRINT,
1899.

"But in his duty prompt at every call,
He watch'd and wept, he pray'd and felt, for all:
And, as a bird each fond endearment tries
To tempt its new-fledg'd offspring to the skies,
He tried each art, reprov'd each dull delay,
Allur'd to brighter worlds, and led the way."
—*Goldsmith.*

PREFACE.

A record like the following needs no apology and but little explanation. It was quite in the historic spirit that this ovation was tendered and accepted. The pastorate which is here honored has one feature that is unique: it is the only pastorate in the history of the Presbyterian Church in Carlisle that has reached the figure of thirty years.

At a meeting of the Board of Trustees, Second Presbyterian Church, Carlisle, Pa., November 14, 1898, it was noted that "our beloved pastor, Rev. Dr. Norcross is about completing thirty years of service in this Church," and it was declared "fitting that this event should be observed and celebrated by the congregation." A committee was then appointed to secure "the proper and suitable observance of said anniversary.

To carry out the considerate purpose of the Board, the co-operation of the Session and all "the different societies of the Church" was sought and obtained. The following pages will remain the permanent memorial of these historical services, and they are now given to the public at the unanimous request of the Board adopted January 23, 1899. At the same meeting "A. G. Miller and D. M. Graham were appointed a committee to act in connection with Dr. Norcross in editing the book."

To carry out the purpose of the congregation a circular letter of invitation and a programme of exercises were prepared, copies of which may be found on the following pages.

CARLISE, PA., March 8, 1899.

The Second Presbyterian Church,

Carlisle, Pa.

Rev. George Norcross, D. D. Pastor.

ELDERS.

Joseph A. Stuart, Andrew Blair,
John A. Means, John C. Eckels,
George McMillen, Wm. B. Beitzel.

DEACONS.

Wm. Scott Coyle, Dalbert W. Houston.

BOARD OF TRUSTEES.

Duncan M. Graham, Esq., President.
Robert C. Lamberton, Secretary.

Walter Stuart, T. J. Parmley,
W. Scott Coyle, Geo. M. Bosler,
W. Chalmers Stuart, A. F. Bedford,
Dr. Thomas Stewart, Robert B. Weaver,
James R. Means, Wm. Graham,
A. G. Miller, Esq., E. J. Gardner,
W. Duncan Green.

GENERAL INVITATION.

You are cordially invited to attend the

ANNIVERSARY SERVICES

to be observed

in connection with the celebration of

THE THIRTY YEARS' PASTORATE

of the

Rev. George Norcross, D. D.,

in the Second Presbyterian Church,

Carlisle, Pennsylvania.

These services will be held on Sabbath,

New Year's Day,

and on Monday, January 2, 1899.

Signed on behalf of the Congregation,

By order of the Committee,

A. G. MILLER,

Chairman.

Carlisle, Pa., December 15, 1898.

1869.   1899.

PROGRAMME.

SABBATH, JANUARY 1, 11 A. M.

ANTHEM—"No Shadows Yonder,"
—Gaul's Holy City.

HISTORICAL SERMON—Rev. Geo. Norcross, D. D.

ANNIVERSARY HYMN—"The Pilgrim Host."

    Now rest, ye pilgrim host
        Look back upon your way,
    The mountains climbed, the torrents crossed.
        Through many a weary day.
    From this victorious height,
        How fair the past appears,
    God's grace and glory shining bright
        On all the bygone years.

"How many at His call,
        Have parted from our throng!
    They watch us from the crystal wall,
        And echo back our song.
    They rest beyond complaints,
        Beyond all sighs and tears;
    Praise be to God for all His saints
        Who wrought in bygone years.

"The banners they upbore
        Our hands still lift on high;
    The Lord they followed evermore
        To us is also nigh.

>   Arise, arise, and tread
>   The future without fears;
>   He leadeth still, whose hand hath led
>   Through all the bygone years.
>
> "When we have reached the home
>   We seek with weary feet.
>   Our children's children still shall come
>   To keep these ranks complete;
>   And He, whose host is one
>   Throughout the countless spheres,
>   Will guide His marching servants on
>   Through everlasting years."

SABBATH, 2.30 P. M.

ANTHEM—"Hark, Hark, My Soul."
—H Rowe Shelley.

HISTORICAL ADDRESS— John Hays, Esq.
  Subject, "Civil Liberty and Presbyterianism."

SABBATH, 7 P. M.

REV. WM. A. WEST, President of Metzger College,
  Presiding.

ADDRESSES.

Rev. J. Agnew Crawford, D. D., Chambersburg, Pa.—
  "The Ministry, the Glory of Christ."

Rev. William H. Logan, Princess Anne, Md.—
  "The Advantages of a Long Pastorate."

Rev. W. T. L. Kieffer, Milton, Pa.—
  "What I Know About This Church and Pastor."

MONDAY, JANUARY 2, 2.30 P. M.

Rev. Ebenezer Erskine, D. D., Presiding.

Anthem,   By the Choir.

ADDRESSES.

Rev. Wm. A. McCarrell, Shippensburg, Pa.—
"The Ideal Church."

Rev. H. G. Stoetzer, Mooredale, Pa.—
"The Pastor's Band."

Rev. Mervin J. Eckels, D. D., Philadelphia, Pa.—
"The Comparative Advantages of Country and City Pastorates."

Rev. Sheldon Jackson, D. D., LL. D., Washington, D. C.—
"Outlook of the Church for the 20th Century."

MONDAY, 7 P. M.

Duncan M. Graham, Esq., President of the Board of Trustees, Presiding.

Musical Selection—"Was it Angels?"
H. W. Porter.

Short Addresses of Congratulation by Hon. R. M. Henderson, Dr. W. M. Frysinger, Dr. H. B. Wile, Rev. A. N. Hagerty, Rev. Geo. H. Bucher, Rev. Robert F. McClean, President Reed and others.

RECEPTION.

For Dr. and Mrs. Norcross, given by the ladies of the congregation in the church parlors.

COMMITTEES.

COMMITTEE FROM BOARD OF TRUSTEES—D. M. Graham, Esq., Chairman; A. G. Miller, Esq., W. Chalmers Stuart, James R. Means, T. J. Parmley, E. J. Gardner and R. B. Weaver, Secretary.

COMMITTEE ON PROGRAMME AND INVITATIONS—A. G. Miller, Esq., Chairman; Major R. H. Pratt, W. Chalmers Stuart, James R. Means, E. J. Gardner, George McMillan, A. F. Bedford, D. W. Houston, R. A. Bucher, Rev. W. A. West and W. Linn McCullough.

COMMITTEE ON FINANCE—Dr. W. Z. Bentz, Chairman; W. Scott Coyle, James R. Means, Frank C. Bosler, T. J. Parmley, W. B. Beitzel, Max Cochran, Dr. S. S. Bishop, Robert H. Royer and Robert M. Stuart.

COMMITTEE ON MUSIC AND DECORATION—Mrs. J. S. Bender, Chairman; Mr. John R. Bland, Choir Master; Mrs. John Hays, Mrs. E. W. Biddle, Mrs. Walter Beall, Mrs. Jas. W. Dale, Miss Jean Richards, Mrs. Thos. A. Harper, Mrs. Wm. Kennedy, Mrs. Jos. McKeehan and Miss Lizzie Halbert, Organist.

COMMITTEE ON RECEPTION AND ENTERTAINMENT—Mrs. S. A. McDowell, Chairman; Mrs. S. J. Beetem, Mrs. Ellen Parker, Mrs. Annie E. Zug, Miss Virginia H. McClellan, Mrs. Wm. Graham, Mrs. John Heber Murray, Mrs. Daniel S. Craighead, Miss Mary E. Bosler, Miss Mary Stuart, Miss Fleta Bosler, Mrs. A. H. Colwell, Mrs. A. A. Thomson, Mrs. Mary L. Biddle and Mrs. E. J. Gardner.

HISTORICAL SERMON
BY THE PASTOR,
REV. GEORGE NORCROSS, D. D.

"That which we have seen and heard declare we unto you."—I. John i: 3.

The religion of the Bible is historical. It is founded on great facts and the testimony of eye-witnesses. Though enemies without and traitors within the Church are doing their best to discredit the historical basis of the Old and New Testaments, these efforts will end in defeat, because the foundation of our holy religion is historic truth. "We have not followed cunningly devised fables," said the great leader of the Apostolic College; and the beloved disciple, John, echoes the same sentiment when he declares in the words of our text, "That which we have seen and heard declare we unto you."

It is true that some men have imagined that a religion disentangled entirely from all historical associations, and commending itself immediately to the soul by its mere intrinsic beauty and excellence, would be an ideal system of devotion. But, whatever might be thought of such a scheme, it would be a gross abuse of words to call it Christianity. That holy religion which was taught by Christ and His apostles was certainly an historical religion—a religion made up of matters of fact, and propounded as historical verities by men who, at the risk of life itself, declared, "We cannot but speak the things which we have seen and heard."

As the cycling ages roll away this testimony of experience is ever increasing. The myriad host who have died in the triumphs of the faith have gone to swell the list of "infallible proofs" that the Church of Christ, which was originally founded on facts, is ever growing more and more by the increase of facts into the divine ideal of that mystical temple of God, which will contain every "living stone" in the eternal plan.

It is the privilege of every worker to add his mite to this ever-increasing collection of facts. To have lived and wrought in the last half of the nineteenth century is no common privilege; to let it pass in "dumb forgetfulness" would be a failure to give God the glory that is due unto His name.

In this spirit of thanksgiving we are here this morning; and, as we raise our stone of Ebenezer, we say devoutly, "Hitherto hath the Lord helped us!" We recall all the way which the Lord our God hath led us, and would say reverently, "That which we have seen and heard declare we unto you."

Five years ago to-day we tried to put on record the history of this particular Church for a quarter of a century. It would be quite useless to repeat the story now. By your courtesy it was committed then carefully to the sure keeping of "the art preservative," and there let it rest. But we have other relations to the Church and the world around us which we must not forget. Let us make a study of these wider relations to-day. Let us recall the history of our times, and see, if possible, what God is teaching by the fast-hurrying events of this nineteenth century, now grown grey and old.

"For I doubt not through the ages one increasing purpose runs,
And the thoughts of men are widened with the process of the suns."

In the affairs of human life there is a time-honored distinction of sacred and secular, or of the holy and profane; and while it may be seriously questioned whether the division is very exact, yet, in a general way, it must be confessed there is, and ought to be, a wide distinction between the Church and the world. The Church as an indwelling, inspiring influence, has much more to do than men generally suppose in shaping the history of the world. Who of us doubts that a reformed Church and an open Bible have given the Anglo-Saxon race for the last two centuries a predominant influence in the politics of the world? Who cannot see that during the same time a corrupt and apostate Church has been like a millstone hanged about the neck of unhappy Spain?

But, without making a digression into the burning questions of the hour, let us follow the lines already indicated, and study

I. The Experiences of the Church during the last half-century.

It is true that this is only a Thirtieth Anniversary, but if we would really understand this period, we must go back a little and estimate the influences already at work.

1. Naturally our first concern is with our own denomination—the Presbyterian Church.

It will soon be two hundred years since the mother Presbytery of Philadelphia was organized. Scattering churches had existed for thirty or forty years before that time. There was one division of the Church during last century, which was healed after a few years of separation. But the saddest division our Church has experienced occurred about sixty years ago.

It so happened under the good providence of God that for a few years my family were connected with the New School branch of the Church; but when in 1844 we removed to the West our lot was cast in the midst of an Old School Church, where I grew up to manhood. Perhaps this personal experience has enabled me to understand the spirit of the two sides better than as though all my relations had been with one party.

The difference of opinion in the Presbyterian Church was not so much over doctrine as polity. It is true that the patience of the Church was sorely taxed by some men who rushed into print with loud professions of improvements in theology and the repudiation of the systems in which they had been taught; but since the smoke of controversy has cleared away this loud outcry seems to have indicated ebullitions of personal conceit rather than serious and general differences in doctrine. The unwise course of such men helped greatly to distract the Church, and they were responsible for the spirit of distrust which so widely prevailed among conservative people.

When, however, the time for reunion came both parties claimed that they accepted the Westminster system in good faith. Honest Presbyterians could hardly have done that, if there had been really much difference of doctrine between the two branches of the American Church.

The real difference had been one of polity or church administration. There had always been a close bond between the Puritan Churches of New England and the Presbyterian Churches of the Middle and Southern States. They both accepted the doctrinal system of the Westminster fathers, but they differed in their methods of church government. The Independent system became dominant in New England, and finally absorbed almost all the Presbyterianism which at one time had settled in that region. We know that a Presbytery of Londonderry existed for forty years, and so numerous were Presbyterians in New England that a Synod was organized, and continued for some time, but was finally absorbed in the State establishment of Congregationalism.

When the streams of influence began to move out toward the West, Independency and Presbytery began to touch in New York, Ohio and other western fields, and then came a curious blending of interests, and often a union of incongruous methods. The New England man had been accustomed to one way of doing things in the church and the Presbyterian had been accustomed to another way. Both knew they were right; neither one would yield much, and so the "conflict of opposing and enduring forces" began, and who could tell where it would end?

In the interest of peace and amity a "Plan of Union" was adopted by the Churches of New England, represented by the Association of Connecticut and the General Assembly of the Presbyterian Church. This proved to be an effort to mix oil and water—only a mechanical union resulted. In the end the "Plan" was repudiated by both parties. But a large number of Churches came into existence, which in polity were neither Congregational nor Presbyterian. They were, however, nominally in the Presbyterian Church, and sent "Committee-men" instead of Elders to the General Assembly.

The Congregational Churches of New England had a system of "Voluntary Societies" for the prosecution of Home and Foreign Mission work. Men who had either grown up in New England, or been educated there, looked upon these societies with favor, but the Presbyterian party came to regard them all with suspicion, as gradually working the disintegration of the Presbyterian Church.

These conditions in the Church developed two pretty clearly defined parties. They began to be known as the New School and the Old School, and as these two parties were nearly balanced there was a sharp struggle for the ascendency in every General Assembly. "During seven years," says Dr. Stearns, "from 1831 to 1837, inclusive, the New School held the majority in that body five times, and their rivals, the Old School, only twice." Threats were made by what seemed to be the dominant party that they had the upper hand, and they were going to keep it.

In this emergency the leaders of the Old School party felt that the Presbyterian Church must be purged of what in their estimation were alien elements. They regarded the "Plan of Union" as the source of all the incongruous matter which had come into the Church, and therefore they thought it not only ill-advised, but an unconstitutional measure. As they mused over the situation they were prepared for heroic treatment of the Church at the next General Assembly.

When the Assembly of 1837 was convened it was found that the Old School party had a majority, and they proceeded to declare the "Plan of Union" unconstitutional, and therefore null and void from the beginning. This action brought out a violent protest, which received an elaborate answer.

The votes on test questions in that Assembly showed that the minority was nearly as large as the majority. As the existing discord between the two parties was felt to be intolerable, it was next proposed to make an amicable division of the Church. Both parties consented to the proposal. An able committee was appointed to devise a plan, but failing to agree as to methods, they asked to be discharged.

The time for radical measures had come. To save the life of the Church the General Assembly decided to amputate the limb that could not be cured, and the four Synods of Western Reserve, Utica, Geneva and Genesee were declared to be "no longer a part of the Presbyterian Church in the United States of America."

The action certainly seemed very severe at the time and there was a loud outcry against it; but the subsequent experiences of the New School party when they were left to work alone with the New England societies showed that it was the only way to peace and safety. For quite a number of years the New School brethren tried loyally to work in the way they had honestly defended, but finally they practically adopted the Old School policy and organized their own boards for Home Mission work, and about the same time the Congregationalists repudiated the "Plan of Union." A good many Churches that had been called nominally Presbyterian dropped all connection with the Presbyterian Church and became Congregational, and so the way was gradually cleared for the reunion in 1869 and 1870 of all the Churches in the North which were in doctrine and polity Presbyterian. It is certainly creditable to both bodies that after mature deliberation this reunion was consummated between them on the basis of the "Standards pure and simple."

The story of this schism in the Presbyterian Church and our recovery from it reminds us of another division which still remains a sad reproach to our Presbsterian name. One of the unfortunate consequences of the slavery agitation was the rupture which it wrought in the Church of Christ. The Methodist Church was divided over the question as early as 1845. The New School branch of the Presbyterian Church divided on the question of slavery in 1857, and the Synods of the South formed themselves into a body called the UNITED SYNOD OF THE PRESBYTERIAN CHURCH."

The division of the Old School Presbyterian Church came with the bursting of the bonds which had held the North and the South together as one united country. For some time it had been the boast of the Old School men that their church was one of the strong ties which helped to maintain the national unity. There was truth in that claim; but how could men remain in one church when they were fighting each other the whole length of the Mason and Dixon's Line? The secession came at last, and so intense were the animosities and prejudices of the time that to this day the unhappy breach has never been healed.

On Dec. 4, 1861, the first General Assembly of the Presbyterian Church in the South was convened at Augusta, Ga. This secession drew off first and last about 700 ministers and 1,200 churches from our connection. A union was formed in 1863 with the New School Synod of the South. This added to the Southern Church about 120 ministers and 190 churches. Since the close of the war there has been steady growth in this Church. It is steadfast for the truth, intensely conservative, full of missionary zeal, and ardent in its attachment for all the old Presbyterian ways. It now numbers 1,448 ministers and 2,873 churches. It is in fraternal relations with our Church, but every effort at reunion has hitherto failed. We know not what surprises the future may have in store for us, but it does seem that a reunion with these brethren in the South must be inevitable in the end.

A matter of peculiar interest to our Church is the system of Pan-Presbyterian Councils, which has been established during my ministry among you. For nearly a quarter of a century there has been a world-wide union of all Presbyterian Churches for mutual encouragement and support. In 1876 the General Assembly entered into the "Alliance of the Reformed Churches throughout the world holding the Presbyterian system."

The first General Council on this basis was held in Edinburg, Scotland, the next year, and your pastor had the honor of being an "Associate Member" of that notable assembly. It was, indeed, an inspiring sight. Here were men from every continent of the globe and from nearly every island of the sea. The castle of Heidelberg was once thought to be the capital of the Reformed Faith, but here were the men of Heidelberg feeling more at home in "Auld Reekie" than they would have done on their own crag overlooking the Neckar.

The Huguenots were once thought to be the leading supporters of their own brother, Calvin, but here was the best that remains of the Huguenots sitting quite at home in Old St. Giles, and uncovering reverently at the grave of John Knox. The world of thought is beginning to realize what it owes to "brave little Holland," whom siege and famine and death could not daunt, in the days when the cruel Spanish Alva sought to crush her to the earth. Many of the brave sons of Dort were there, and held an honored place in this, the first Council of the Reformed Faith.

It was more than three hundred years since Cranmer, the Archbishop of Canterbury, wrote to John Calvin, proposing a union of all the Reformed Churches. In this letter he said: "Our adversaries are now holding their Councils at Trent, for the establishment of their errors; and shall we neglect to call together a godly Synod, for the refutation of error, and for restoring and propagating the truth?"

To this proposal Calvin replied most cordially, and declared that to accomplish such a purpose he "would not grudge to cross ten seas." Poor, short-sighted men! They did not think that after three hundred years the English Church would not be reformed enough to be interested in such a gathering met for the promotion of a Scriptural faith and polity; but would be looking back mournfully to the good old times when the Church was not reformed at all.

But all this recalls some interesting events in the history of the English Church during this last half century. After being one of the great bulwarks of Protestantism for more than three hundred years, many of her most illustrious sons seem to be ashamed of her past record. A wonderful revolution has been going on in the life-time of some of us here present. The Erastianism which once satisfied at least the High Churchman now satisfies him no longer. There is a loud cry for Church reform. By that one class means changes that would approach Presbyterianism, but another class means the imitation of Romanism. The average Churchman has waked up to the fact that the English Establishment has long been dominated over by the State in a way that is dishonoring to Christ and His cause.

But to a loyal Presbyterian the Churchman's zeal on this subject often takes an amusing form. We can hardly understand how a man in this age of the world could be willing to go to jail for the privilege of conforming his worship to a fashion set by the Roman apostasy. At this time in the world's history, it seems rather amusing to find a young minister honestly considering whether a clergyman is not bound to be a celibate, whether monkery would not be a good thing after all, whether the Reformation of the 16th Century was not a mistake, whether it would not be advisable to strike the word "Protestant" out of the name of the Church of England. Can you imagine the amused interest or indignant scorn with which John Calvin would have regarded Mr. Gladstone's act of interviewing the Pope to know whether the orders of the English Church were valid or not? I think the little tractate which the great reformer would have written on the subject would have made very interesting reading.

Well, well, it is not our affair, but in taking a glance at all the world we can hardly be blamed for noticing an institution that looms up as large as the Established Church of England. After all we can not believe that the sturdy sense of the English people will succumb to the follies of these reactionists. The sensible people in the establishment will find themselves helped by the strong evangelical spirit of the Dissenters, and England will never lose her place as the bulwark of Protestantism.

But surely this hasty review of the Church would not be complete without noticing the singular fortunes of that venerable system which accepts as its Head the Pope of Rome. To the theologian or the student of Church History, the Church of Rome has in our day made two conspicuous advances in that downward course which began with the subtle movement of "THE MYSTERY OF INIQUITY" which the Apostle Paul noted as already working in his day.

One of these new departures for the worse was the adoption by the Church of an old speculation concerning the "Immaculate Conception of the Virgin Mary," the other was the adoption of the dogma concerning "the Supremacy and Infallibility of the Pope."

The doctrine of the Immaculate Conception of the Virgin Mary, which means that she was born perfectly free from the taint of Original Sin, was much debated from the 12th to the 14th Century. In other words, it was an open question, even among the faithful, and it remained so until the 8th of December, 1854, when this new article was added to the creed of the Roman Church. St. Bernard, St. Thomas Aquinas, the Dominicans, and many more had opposed the doctrine as unscriptural and unreasonable; but Pope Pius IX having sent a circular to all the bishops of his Church throughout the world, and having obtained the assent of a large majority of them, publicly declared this monstrous heresy to be a doctrine of the Church, and every good Catholic must believe it now on pain of damnation.

The dogma of the Pope's Infallibility was also an advance on the former position of the Roman Church on this subject. She had never claimed more than that the Church was infallible. Some held that this infallibility resided in a Council, some that it was in the Pope, while others thought that it was in both united. But in 1870 the Vatican Council promulgated the doctrine of the Pope's Infallibility in all its bald offensiveness, though it was opposed by many at that time in good standing in the Church. It resulted in a schism in the Roman Communion, and the formation of the "Old Catholic Church," under the lead of the great scholar, Doellinger.

To many Protestant minds this dogma filled the cup of that Apostasy which St. Paul predicted would come in the Church of God, and completed the picture of "the man of sin" who would exalt himself, "so that he, as God, sitteth in the temple of God, showing himself that he is God" (2 Thess. ii. 4).

Students of prophecy had long predicted that the latter part of this century would witness overwhelming changes in that great Apostasy foretold as coming in the Church of God. It is a curious fact that as soon as this dogma of the Pope's Infallibility was promulgated, the Emperor of the French was compelled to withdraw his forces from Rome, where they had kept the Pope on his throne of temporal authority. As the French went out, the army of united

Italy, under Victor Emmanuel, came in, and the Infallible Pope retired before his loving children to the Vatican, where he has been playing at "prisoner's base" ever since.

It is also interesting to note that the cause of haste on the part of the Emperor, Louis Napoleon, in withdrawing his troops from the support of the "Holy Father" was the threatened avalanche from Protestant Germany, where the Lutheran King of Prussia was furbishing his sword for that conflict, which, in a short time, crowned him in the palace of Versailles the Emperor of United Germany. Surely he must be blind who cannot see in all this the finger of God.

Did time permit, it would be very interesting to review more at length the progress of the Church at large. Even the very conservative Greek Church has been considerably modified by Evangelical missionaries from the West.

The Lutheran Church of Germany has in a measure recovered from the palsy of Rationalism, which rested like an incubus upon it during the first half of this century. Our brethren, the Waldenses, have entered on a career of evangelization throughout the whole extent of Italy, and are now as much petted as they were once persecuted by the House of Savoy.

The Evangelical Churches of this country are striving with generous emulation to take the land for Christ, and are more than ever inclined to magnify the fundamentals in which they agree and to minify the non-essentials in which they differ. A spirit of missionary zeal has taken possession of every branch of the Church, which promises the speedy evangelization of our lost world. The signs that "the morning cometh" are so bright that we seem to hear the Spirit of God saying to a tempest-tossed Church, "Look up, and lift up your heads; for your redemption draweth nigh."

II. But now turning to the more secular aspects of history, let us review the events which have crowded the last half of this Century.

Some of you will remember the rejoicings in 1850 over the Compromise Measures by Congress, which it was hoped would bring peace to the country then dangerously agitated over the question of slavery. The history of the next ten years showed that the subject of slavery could not be kept out of politics. The national conscience was not at ease, and could not be quieted by any kind of compromise; while the friends of "the patriarchal institution" were defending their practice of slave-holding by the example of Abraham, Isaac and Jacob, as the champions of polygamy in Utah are doing to-day. These fiery spirits at the South were getting more indignant every day over their imaginary wrongs, and finally the Presidential election in 1860 was made the pretext for precipitating on the country all the horrors of a civil war.

The people had become accustomed to sectional threats, but many thought them idle vaporings only intended for political effect. The apathy of the country under the reports of treasonable movements in the South now seems almost incredible. But all this was suddenly changed when the infatuation of treason fired on Fort Sumter. Suddenly the North rose up like a young giant awaked out of sleep. The indignation at this insult to the national flag knew no bounds. It swept like a flame from Maine to California, and all party ties were consumed before it.

This generation can never forget the anxieties, the sufferings, the sorrows, the awful bereavements of the next five years culminating in the tragic death of him whom the great mass of the people had come to trust and love as the father of his country.

It will be impossible to follow the fortunes of the fight during all those weary years. But what need is there? You can read them to-day in the scars which those events cut deep and during on your own hearts.

To the people of Carlisle, however, the struggle assumed an awful significance when finally the tide of war came sweeping near their homes. Many of you remember the alarms of that quiet summer when the storm of conflict burst in upon your peaceful valley and the thunder of artillery demanded the surrender of this ancient and honorable borough, and the time-honored buildings at the Garrison were wrapt in flames, and the flying shells were screaming high in the air over homes that had never known the fright of war before. A few of you can remember the far away boom of that terrific cannonade, which around the neighboring town of Gettysburg was settling for us all the uncertain question of national destiny. Who of you then living can ever forget the agony of those days? You did not know then, as we do now, that the waves of rebellion had reached their highest water mark that fateful summer. But so it was, and as we stand on the summit of the National Cemetery at Gettysburg where President Lincoln pronounced his immortal eulogy over those dead heroes who had given their lives for the unity of the nation, we see in imagination the crest of that wave of frantic rebellion as it rises in Pickett's desperate charge, and breaks at the feet of the boys in blue, and sinks away in hopeless repulse.

There was serious work still to be done, for the demon of sectional hate was hard to cast out. But the Federal forces had found a leader in "the greatest Captain of the age." It was said of the reticent Von Moltke that "he could hold his tongue in nine languages." General Grant was undoubtedly the equal of the great German both in genius and reticence. In the deep dark shades of the "Wilderness" the fight went on for awhile; but at last even the gallant leader of the "Lost Cause," Gen. Robert E. Lee, the darling of the South, gave the signal for surrender—the two great chiefs met with every mark of courtesy and consideration at Appomattox Court House, such terms of capitulation were agreed on as even the South pronounced generous and honorable, and the War of the Great Rebellion was over.

In the awful heats of that conflict were melted the shackels of a race of bondmen, and God solved the problem of slavery, which had proved too hard for our statesmen. It is His prerogative to overrule evil for good, and it is quite remarkable how the whole country has recovered its sense of unity, and how the men, who once stood glaring at each other in the deadly strife of battle now sit around the same camp-fires in friendly converse, and live over again the stirring scenes of that awful time.

We have scarcely heard the sound of fife and drum again, except in gala day procession, until that dull, heavy explosion under the Maine in the treacherous harbor of Havana aroused the nation from its selfish lethargy, and reminded us all that a people capable of such a wanton act of cruel perfidy could not be trusted in the commonwealth of nations with the care of a subject people reduced to the point of starvation by oppression and misgovernment.

Perhaps never in the history of the world was an army gathered in such hot haste. Men needed no urging to enlist; for their blood was up, and even the children wanted to fight the Spaniards. In a Summer of unusual heat, men were eager to invade the tropical climate of Cuba, and face the deadly malaria of festering swamps and dare the poisonous breath of the yellow fever, and fight the dastard race who, from the days of the Spanish Armada, had sought the downfall of Anglo-Saxon civil and religious liberty.

Suddenly, like thunder-bolts out of heaven, the vengeance of a free people fell on the forces of Spain, where they hovered like eagles gathered about the carcass of a dying people half the world apart. Certainly, never before in the history of the world were two such naval victories won as that in the Bay of Manila, which has made the name of Dewey famous forever, and that which crowned the exciting chase and capture of Cervera's fleet as it escaped from the narrow-mouthed Harbor of Santiago de Cuba, only to be sunk and destroyed in the blue waters of the Caribbean Sea.

The wisest of all our public men cannot tell exactly what the outcome of all this will be. But the treaty of peace has been signed at Paris, and the heel of the oppressor and the thumb-screw of the Inquisition have been removed forever from these prostrate Islands, and the door is opened wide for the entrance of light and liberty to these benighted people, whom the Lord has thus brought out of the darkness, and the shadow of death, and has broken their bands asunder. May God give to the American people the wisdom which is needed in these high affairs!

But wars are by no means the most important events in national history. They have a wonderful power to arrest the eye, to quicken the pulse, to fire the imagination, and they are often used as God's hammer to shatter hoary abuses; but after all, war plays but a small part in the real story of nations; let us turn, then, to the triumphs of peace.

It is difficult to speak in sober terms of the discoveries, inventions and improvements of the last fifty years. They have silently changed the intellectual and social life of the civilized world. To the men of a former generation, the story of these triumphs of physical science would have sounded like the tales of the Arabian Nights; to the spirit of the Middle Ages they would have seemed the work of the Black Art. It is not wonderful that their success has sometimes turned the heads of scientists and made them dream that man is independent of God. Men have not always had the reverence of Joseph Henry in approaching the thunder cloud of natural forces, who said to his assistant in electrical experiments, "Uncover your head now, for I am about to ask God a question."

But already the fever of excitement seems to have passed, and many of these men are acknowledging "the sweet reasonableness" of religion, and verifying the wise opinion of Bacon, that while a little philosophy inclines men to Atheism, depth in philosophy brings them back to religion.

We can hardly trust ourselves to speak of the development of our own country. We look on with amazement, and can only say, What hath God wrought? Who lifted the veil from the vista of the misty future, and showed the prophet that the time might come when a nation should be born in a day?

Those of us who are in the afternoon of life can remember when the Mississippi river was the somewhat indefinite boundary of our Western settlements, and all beyond was the Great American Desert and the Rocky Mountains. This was before Whitman stayed the hand of our diplomats at Washington, and saved to the Stars and Stripes the land which the poet of that day described as

> "The continuous woods,
> Where rolls the Oregon, and hears no sound
> Save his own dashings—yet the dead are there!
> And millions in those solitudes, since first
> The flight of years began, have laid them down
> In their last sleep—the dead reign there alone!"

Well, the wand of the magician, or, better still, the breath of God, has passed over the scene, and the reign of death has been invaded, and now the living are there.

Some of us can remember the day when Thomas H. Benton stood in the United States Senate urging on his somewhat incredulous hearers the claims of his scheme for the construction of a railway to the Pacific Coast. In mind's eye now, we can see the old hero as, with dexter finger pointing toward sunset, he exclaimed dramatically, "There lies the East!" How little did he dream that before the century would close a half-dozen lines of steel rails would bind the Pacific Slope to the Atlantic Coast.

But the time fails me to tell all that I intended along these lines of material progress. The mind of man has been busy with the problems of nature in the heavens above and the earth beneath. We have seen space shortened and time annihilated. We have seen the lightning caught and harnessed to the car of man, fastened at the crossings of the streets to turn his midnight into day, or sent, like swift angels, to carry his message over river and mountain and down through the awful depths of "the sounding sea."

And finally, perhaps most wonderful of all, by the mysterious circuits of this unseen agent, man hears the voice of his brother half across the continent, and thus the possibilities of human utterance are multiplied ten thousand fold.

But, during these later years man has not been satisfied with triumphs over nature; he has also set about recovering as much as possible what has been lost through the ravages of time. The spirit of historical research has been very much quickened by the discovery of priceless manuscripts, the deciphering of lost languages, and the uncovering of buried cities. The spade of the archæologist has been richly rewarded by the spoils of lost art, the clear record of old inscriptions, and the pompous details of dead empires. How happy is the antiquary as he turns over the stone leaves of this ancient history, deciphers the clay tablets which have survived the ruin of empires, and thus rescues from the maw of oblivion the story of the past.

Many other events of the past few years crowd upon us as worthy of honorable mention, but I may not tax your patience longer in this direction. However, before we close the book, you may be ready to ask, What do you think the most impressive lessons of our period? What has God been teaching us by His providences? Well, to that I would say,

1. The most impressive lesson of our times is, that the Christian religion carries with it the blessing of God.

The Christian nations stand in the forefront of national power and progress; and all the world begins to see it. The domination of the world has fallen into the hands of three or four great powers, and these powers are all Christian; and all the world is saying, What made these lands so great?

Japan, for example, wants to know the secret of the progress in the Western nations. She begins to see that it is the religion of these nations that lays the foundation for their masterful greatness. She sends her bright young men to America, to England, to France, to Germany, that they may learn the secret of our Western civilization. In the great universities noisy skeptics try to put them on the wrong trail, but all in vain. These young men see that the Code of Moses and the Sermon on the Mount are the foundation stones on which alone national greatness can be built, and they go back to tell the story.

Even China, with all her stupid conservatism, begins to see it—yes, and to hear it, too, in the roar of the guns which her smart young rival, Japan, so audaciously has trained upon her ports. Egypt and Palestine, India and the Isles of the Sea, are all waking up to the idea that the mighty God of battles is with the Christian nations.

In the long run, a nation governed by the principles of the Koran cannot cope with one saturated with the truths of the Bible. The lazy quietism of Buddha cannot compete with the tireless activity of the Son of the Carpenter. The car of Juggernaut is not the car of progress. Even a nation which gives half its days to the veneration of the Saints is found to be no match for one that accepts as the law of God, "Six days shalt thou labor and do all thy work; but the seventh day is the Sabbath of the Lord thy God: in it thou shalt not do any work."

In other words, pure religion has the promise not only of the future life, but of that which must be lived in this work-day world. Man may imagine that he can improve on the law of God, but the issue shows that he is badly mistaken. God is teaching by the fate of nations what He has ordained as the everlasting principles of sound religion for the human race; and one of the hopeful signs of a coming Millenium is, that the world is beginning to see that the blessing of God abides with those who honor His Son, Jesus Christ.

2. Another important lesson which God is teaching in our day is, that the Church is most successful when independent of the State.

In those early days of apostolic fervor and simplicity, to which all the Church looks back as upon the whole the most successful period of her history, the Church expected no help from the State, and was most happy when she was left alone, even in contemptuous neglect. It was then that, full of faith and the Holy Ghost, she swept over the known world and planted the cross in every corner of the Roman Empire.

But with her great success came entangling alliances with the State. It was a proud day for the Church when the Emperor Constantine espoused her cause, and called the Council of Nice to settle her faith. But imperial favor was by no means an unmixed good, and the Church has been slow to learn that when she is weak then is she strong, that she cannot safely accept any Head but her Adorable Redeemer, and that though kings may be her "nursing fathers," their help may be given in such a way as to palsy her noblest testimony for her Divine Lord and Master.

One of the great lessons which God is teaching in our land seems to be that the Church not only does not need the help of the State, but is far more successful without it. Many plausible arguments may be made in favor of political patronage for the Church. It sounds very pious that kings should be "nursing fathers," and that the State should make a profession of religion, and that a Christian nation must support the Christian Church; but sad experience has taught us that the conquering chariot of Christ cannot be "hitched" to the "star" of any earthly power, however imperial it may be in glorious majesty.

The experience of America has shown that the Church is best served by the State when she is left free from political patronage, and dependent on those who accept her teaching, love her worship, and desire the extension of her benign influence.

This old question is one of importance, even at the present time, for, though a pure American Church does not ask for State help in any way, a corrupt Church is not only ready to take it, but is constantly plotting raids on the public treasury, and seeking to extend her power through corrupt, political influence.

The Roman hierarchy indeed makes loud professions of only wanting "an open field and no favor;" but the fact remains that Rome is as ready as ever to take public money to support her schools and her charities, to say nothing of her imposing temples which she loves to exhibit in conspicuous places in every city. All our public men are beset with her cajoleries and threatened with her vengeance if they fail to do her bidding. May the American people never forget that "the price of liberty is eternal vigilance!"

3. Now closely related to all this is another lesson which God is teaching,—and that is the need of toleration and charity.

By this I do not mean that pseudo-charity which is ready to take the devil under its patronage, and allows the altars of Moloch to be built "fast by the oracle of God," but the charity which is quick to note the lineaments of Christ and is ready to receive all those who bear His divine likeness.

One of the most brilliant writers of our day has called attention to the fact, that God by His Providence has compelled the modern world to learn the lesson of toleration by making human existence intolerable while Catholic and Protestant sought to exterminate each other. It is not that now they mutually accept each other's systems, but that they have learned to tolerate each other, and live together as good neighbors.

If I rightly judge the signs of the times, God in His Providence is compelling this kind of toleration along many different lines. He is making it more impossible every day that any one branch of His Church can ever again dominate the world. It does not seem to be His plan that any one denomination like Aaron's rod should ultimately swallow up all the rest. God is working out a wonderful problem for His Church and the world in this unique land of ours, and one result will be the discovery of what true church unity is. Men will learn in the end that spiritual unity is the divine ideal, and this has always been consistent with considerable diversity. Long ago the apostle assured us that "there are differences of administrations, but the same Lord," and when the Church accepts that as true, the dream of outward organic unity will end.

As Christians we all expect a brighter day to dawn for the Church of God, but the more successful the Church is and the larger she grows, the more absolutely unwieldly will be the body if it must all be compressed into one outward, visible organization. For one I do not believe God ever intended anything of the kind. I look for unity in diversity, and the American Church springing from many historical germs is working out the problem for the world.

In one sense the Church never seemed so divided as in our land, but the division is more seeming than real. In many cases our separate organizations are little more than a division of the labor to be done for the kingdom of God. We do not repudiate each other. We do not war against each other as the devil is constantly asserting. On the contrary we publish it from every pulpit that the Church of God is one. We show it in all our union work; we confess it by pulpit exchanges where the Church is truly reformed; we mingle our tears and prayers around the common table of our Lord, and then rise up and tell the reviler of the sacramental host of God's elect that all Christians are one.

4. Another lesson which God has been teaching impressively in our times is, that He has the control over all the forces of nature, and all the hearts of men to carry out His own plans.

It is not hard for theists to believe that back of all the stellar worlds and behind all the forces of nature there is a first great Cause, who is not only unsearchable in His judgments, but inscrutable in His ways of working. Even Matthew Arnold believed that this world is so organized as to "make for righteousness." But the thoughtful Christian may go farther than this, and say with the firmest conviction of faith,—"All things work together for good to them that love God."

Those who believe in the promises of divine revelation expect a glorious future for a redeemed world. There is an optimism of faith which, with a divine warrant, expects this poor, sin-cursed earth to be filled with the knowledge and glory of God as the waters cover the sea. The people who entertain such high hopes are not surprised when they find God so overruling in past history that gunpowder is discovered when it is necessary to put the serf on an equality with his feudal lord; and the mariner's compass is invented, when God is ready to have the New World uncovered as an asylum for His persecuted Church; and the art of printing is exploited, when He means to have His Word distributed and studied at every hearth-stone; and steam navigation comes, when He means that "many shall run to and fro, and knowledge shall be increased;" and new explosives of more deadly power are discovered, when He intends to make the enginery of war so deadly that even the greatest war-captains of the age shall begin to cry out for peace.

Now we can see that it is along such lines as these that God works and unfolds His plans. In all this we can see the hand of God in the past; but the same is true in our own times. Every labor-saving machine, every economic device, every crafty invention, every scientific discovery, will be found in the end to hasten on the blessed day of Peace which God has promised.

It is hard for men to believe it; but God is governing the world on a prearranged plan, of which He is the author and the finisher. It is not that man is left with nothing to do—quite the reverse. God's plan is that the holy temple of His Church shall be built by the men of His own choice, and that the work shall be done even in troublous times, and that men shall have the privilege of carrying on this holy enterprise with grand heroic sacrifices, which shall give them fellowship with Christ in His sufferings. Every private that struggled up the hill in the face of shot and shell to take the defences of Santiago last Summer had the consciousness of comradeship and fellowship with the Commander-in-Chief of all our armies. And so it is in the conquest of this world for Christ. Every private in the army hears the gracious words of his great Captain assuring him "Ye are My friends, if ye do whatsoever I command you." He is the great Captain of our salvation, and all His true followers feel themselves honored to be called by His name, and they would go to the death for Him.

But it is hard for men to believe that the man who allowed himself to be crucified between two thieves now sits on the mediatorial throne of the universe, and is upholding all things by the word of His power, and is working out the problems of redemption according to the counsel of His own will, and that His kingdom at last shall fill the earth and embrace the race.

But now God is teaching just this impressive lesson to those who have ears to hear. He is showing us that He is abundantly able to take care of His own. He assures us in His Word that He is overturning and overturning in the affairs of this world until He shall " come whose right it is," and then " He shall have dominion from sea to sea and from the river unto the ends of the earth." The silver and the gold are His, and the cattle on a thousand hills. When they are needed they are brought and laid down as tribute at His feet. The doors may seem shut and bolted, but when the fullness of time has come the doors fly open wide and the King of glory marches in, not, indeed, to the sound of drum and trumpet, for His kingdom cometh not with observation, but in the person of His humble missionaries, who begin the task of uplifting the lowliest, knowing that if we elevate the lowest strata of society we shall lift it all.

Our blessed Lord blamed the men of His day because they did not study the signs of the times. God forbid that we should fall into the same condemnation! We must not only study the Book of Nature and the Book of Providence, but the Book of Divine Revelation, to know what God has in store for His Church. Let us be careful that we are not taken by surprise as were His people of old when the greatest glory of their race "suddenly came to His temple." We are rapidly sweeping on to the consummation of all things, to that

> "One far-off divine event,
> To which the whole creation moves"

May the Lord open our eyes, that we may understand His Word, and hear Him saying, "Can ye not discern the signs of the times?"

HISTORICAL ADDRESS,

CIVIL LIBERTY AND PRESBYTERIANISM,

BY

JOHN HAYS, ESQ.

The invitation to address you came with the right to select a subject. The subject should accord with the purpose of these services. They are to show our appreciation of a pastorate over this Presbyterian church for nearly the one-half of its sixty-six years of existence. It would seem appropriate, therefore, to consider, from a Layman's standpoint, some of the great steps leading up to the Establishment of Civil and Religious Liberty, as shown by the Form of Government of the United States and of the Presbyterian Church, with a glance at any distinguishing feature in this Church, its Founders, and its local prominence and influence.

In these closing years of the nineteenth century it is impossible to form a just conception of the condition of the people at the time Europe began to emerge from the darkness of the Middle Ages. One writer says of it:

"It should be known that there are three condi-
"tions of men in this world: the first is, that of
"gentlemen; and the second is, that of such as are
"naturally free, being born of a free mother; * *
"* * the third estate of men is, that of such as
"are not free; and these are not all of one condi-
"tion, for some are so subject to their lord that he
"may take all they have, alive or dead, and im-
"prison them whenever he pleases, being account-
"able to none but God; while others are treated
"more gently, from whom their lord can take noth-
"ing but customary payments, though at their death
"all they have escheats to him" (1).

This subjection to temporal lords was bad enough, but there was another which was far worse. It embraced all three of the classes named, and it was the subjection of all to the power and exactions of the so-called Church and Ministers of God.

A writer says of these Ministers of God:

"Practically they alone baptized and married peo-
"ple (though unmarried themselves). They had the

---

(1) Beaumenoir—as quoted by Hallam in "Middle Ages," Vol. 1, pp. 196-198 and 199.

"charge of men on their death beds; they alone
"buried, and could refuse christian burial in the
"churchyards. They regulated the disposition of
"the goods of deceased persons. When a man
"made a will it had to be proven in their Eccle-
"siastical Courts. If men disputed their claims,
"doubted their teaching, or rebelled from their doc-
"trines, they virtually condemned them to the
"stake, by handing them over to the civil power,
"which acted in submission to their dictates (1).

A Catholic writer says:

"I see that we can scarcely get anything from
"Christ's ministers but for money; at baptism,
"money; at bishoping, money; at marriage, money:
"for confession, money;—no, not extreme unction
"without money. They will ring no bells without
"money; so that it seemeth that Paradise is shut up
"from them that have no money. The rich is bur-
"ied in the Church, the poor in the churchyard.
"The rich man may marry with his nearest kin,
"but the poor not so, albeit he be ready to die for
"love of her. The rich may eat flesh in Lent but
"the poor may not, albeit fish perhaps is much

---

(1). F. Seebohm,—"The Protestant Revolution," p. 9, in "Epochs of Modern History."

"dearer. The rich man may readily get large in-
"dulgences, but the poor none, because he wanteth
"money to pay for them." (1).

Still another writer says:

"They have their tenth part of all the corn,
"meadows, pasture, grass, wood, colts, calves, lambs,
"geese and chickens. Over and besides the tenth
"part of every servant's wages, wool, milk, honey
"wax, cheese and butter; yea, and they look so nar-
"rowly after their profits that the poor wife must
"be countable to them for every tenth egg, or else
"she geteth not her rights at Easter, and shall be
"taken as a heretic." (2).

They held the learning and the learned of the world,—binding unto themselves and for their own purposes those who were not of their own number by the privileges and protection accorded them. Thus they required that criminals against the law of the land, who could read and write, should be turned over to their Ecclesiastical Courts where they could be set free and defy the law. All learn-

---

(1) Juan De Valdez quoted by F. Seebohm in "The Protestant Revolution," in "Epochs of Modern History," p. 57-8.

(2) Quoted by F. Seebohm in "The Protestant Revolution" in "Epochs of Modern History," p. 58.

ing, including the Word of God, was covered up in the Latin language that the people might not comprehend it. (1).

These ecclesiastics " became the lawyers and dip- " lomatists, ambassadors, Ministers, chancellors and even prime ministers of princes." (2).

A long line of Cardinal Dukes ruled in the name of Kings and Princes over almost every country in Europe. They encouraged their nominal masters, and shared in their sinful pleasures, in defiance of all laws,—civil or religious. They oppressed the people and waxed mighty in wickedness.

And yet from this cruel oppression, as we look back, from our present standpoint, over the teeming years as they rolled by, it seems to have been the divine purpose to lead the people out of and up to a Republican form of Government in the State and in the Church as surely as the children of Israel were led out of the oppression of Egypt and up to the promised land.

It required the boldest and most adventurous of many lands to form the admixture known as the

(1) F. Seebohm in "The Protestant Revolution" in " Epochs of Modern History," pp. 11 and 12

(2) F. Seebohm, in "The Protestant Revolution " in " Epochs of Modern History," p. 10.

Anglo-Saxon race. It resulted from successive conquests, and not from design on part of the mixing elements. The oppression of the people was like unto a grinding between the upper and the nether millstone. To the Anglo-Saxons it was intolerable. They rebelled, and under the leadership of their Barons, as the "Army of God," (1) they wrested, in 1215, from their King, for the "community of the whole land," "Magna Charta" (2)—the Great Charter of Liberty—whose principles are to-day embodied in the Constitution and laws of every English-speaking people, and furnish sure protection in the "enjoyment of life, liberty and the pursuit of happiness."

This was the *first great step* in the advance towards Civil Liberty.

A century later—in 1315—some of the Swiss Cantons successfully rebelled against their rulers, and in time formed a confederacy for mutual protection, with the motto inscribed upon its flag, "Each for all and all for each" (3).

It seems now as if that confederacy had been ex-

---

(1) History of the English People—Green, Vol. 1, page 243.
(2) History of the English People—Green, Vol. 1, page 244.
(3) F. Seebohm, in "The Protestant Revolution" in "Epochs of Modern History, pp. 58 and 59.

pressly designed as a future haven of refuge for the persecuted and exiled Anglo-Saxon reformers, and where, in perfect safety, the most complete "Institutes of the Christian Religion" could be published to the world (1).

There were universities throughout Europe—some thirty or forty of them—in more or less close connection with each other. They were the great centres of the learned world and the oldest and most celebrated of them were Oxford and Cambridge, in England. Students passed from one to another, and wherever they went, carried with them the laboriously written books considered new and important (2). But the learning and the books were in Latin. The scholars were controled by the Ecclesiastics. They were bound to them by self interest. Yet in little more than half a century after the haven of refuge had been provided for in Switzerland, an honest, learned and fearless man, who had passed through the University of Oxford, had become a Professor of Theology and was there lecturing to and writing for thousands of students.

---

(1) Geneva did not come into the confederacy until 1815 but achieved freedom in 1530.

(2) F. Eeebohm, in "The Protestant Revolution" in "Epochs of Modern History," pp. 13 and 14.

He was, as a late writer says, "the first Reformer "who dared, when deserted and alone, to question "and deny the creed of the Christendom around him, "to break through the tradition of the past, and "with his last breath, to assert the freedom of relig- "ious thought against the dogmas of the Papacy.(1).

His students carried his teachings and his writings, in Latin, of course, to other Universities in Europe. Their doctrine was unknown and astounding to the Ecclesiastics of those days. They were subversive of their power over the people, and opened the way for a religion of the heart and conscience. The better to reach the people, he threw aside the Latin language and taught and wrote in the Midland dialect of England. He set on foot a body of poor Preachers, called "Simple Priests," whose common dress, bare feet and coarse sermons accomplished a work that no other means could have effected (2).

To some extent, perhaps, the "Peasants' Revolt," under Wat. Tyler in 1381, is attributable to their teachings. Terribly suppressed as it was after a promise to comply with the demands made, yet it

---

(1) "History of the English People," Green—Vol. 1, p. 446.
(2) "History of the English People," Green—Vol. 1, p. 474.

accomplished its purpose, for slavery of English people quietly died away (1).

Certain it is, however, that the teachings of this Doctor of Theology and his " Simple Priests," produced the " Lollards " as they were derisively called, who, as Hallam says, " aided by the conflu-
" ence of foreign streams, swelled into the Protest-
" ant Church of England." (2)

As life drew to its close, an earlier translation of the Bible, made with the assistance of one of his scholars, was revised. Numerous copies of it were written and distributed. Chaucer, his friend and contemporary, the father of English Poetry, wrote in the same dialect. " These two," as a modern writer says, " little knew that they were laying the "foundations, as it were, of the strongest and most
" vigorous language ever used by human beings for
" the expression of their thoughts, but it has become
" the English language of the nineteenth century,—
" the language of liberty." (3)

With his life work done, this Doctor of Theology, —John Wyckliff,—was, in 1384, laid away in the

---
(1) "History of the English People," Green—Vol. 1 p. 486.
(2) Hallam's "Constitutional History of England," vol. 1 page 70.
(3) Coffin's "Story of Liberty," page 51.

grave, and the FIRST GREAT STEP TOWARDS RELIGIOUS FREEDOM had been taken. The people had gotten hold of the truth and the learning of the Universities was thenceforth to be used for their good and to the glory of God. Yet, in childish spite, the maddened Ecclesiastics, forty-four years after the death of Wyckliff, dug up his bones, burned them and cast the ashes upon a stream running down to the sea, as if in that way they could drown out the everlasting truths he taught.

Events after Wyckliff's death, in the opening out of the advance towards republicanism in Church and State, followed each other in rapid succession. John Huss, in far-off Bohemia, was then only eleven years old. He became a learned scholar in Theology, an eloquent preacher, and a prolific writer. Thoroughly conversant with the teachings of Wyckliff, he not only believed them, but gave publicity to their doctrines in his writings and sermons. He ranged himself on the side of truth, and because he would not yield up the faith that was in him he was burned at the stake in 1415. Jerome, but little younger than Huss, distributed throughout Bohemia Wyckliff's writings, became the friend and follower of Huss, and in 1416, like him, was burned at the stake. A crusade was proclaimed against their followers, and from that crusade, as Motley says (1), "Many Netherlanders came back, feeling more sympathy with the heresy which they had attacked than with the Church for which they battled."

The sympathy thus brought back from Bohemia prepared the Dutch to receive the truth gladly, and to hold fast to it throughout the butchery they were to be subjected to. What is true of the Dutch is true also to some extent of the French and Germans. The seed that Wyckliff sowed was swelling into life and growth.

Thus the "Simple Priests"—Wyckliff's publishers—and the followers of Huss were circulating the new doctrines and scriptural knowledge in the West and in the East. Intolerance and persecution were given a new impetus. Prior to that time they had nothing to feed upon but the handful of Waldenses, whose faith with themselves was locked up in the northern mountains of Italy. But now the income of the ecclesiastics, as well as their power, was threatened. True, they had, as it is said, one-third of all the lands, and their revenues were princely, apart from the tithes given them by law,

---
(1) The Dutch Republic, Vol. 1, page 71—Introduction.

and the donations extorted through fear, but if these pernicious doctrines prevailed, there would be an end to revenue from selling indulgences, from baptism, marriage, confession, death, burial, prayers for the dead, and the numerous sources of income to the crowds of minor ecclesiastics—there would be an end to their ownership of human souls.

Judgment was therefore passed upon the holders of the new doctrines. They were adjudged to be heretics—enemies of God and man—and sentenced to death in all the horrible ways that cruel ingenuity could devise. Fiercely and brutally that sentence was carried out against the Lollards, the Hussites, and those who followed after them. History is blood-red with details of it.

But the publishers and the laboriously written books of that day were inadequate. Then, as always, the needed instrument in the Lord's work was provided. In 1423,—eight years after John Huss was burned and before the ashes of Wyckliff's bones were cast upon the water,—Lawrens Coster, of Haarlem, carved letters upon wood, tied them together in words and printed from them. (1) Johann Gutenburg, a workman, is said to have derived

---

(1) Coffin's "Story of Liberty," p. 70.

his idea from these wooden letters and experimenting with them, after some years, with help from Johann Faust, perfected a metal and mould for type in 1450 (1). Six years thereafter "he completed " the printing of the Bible in Latin" (2). It was for the learned and the learned used it. The instrument was provided and THE SECOND GREAT STEP, IN THE UPWARD ADVANCE, TOWARDS CIVIL AND RELIGIOUS LIBERTY, had been taken."

But the little haven of refuge in the mountains of Switzerland, designed, as it seems, for some future leaders, will never answer for the hosts to follow their leadership, and a place must be found where the coming army of people can find a refuge, and where great problems can be worked out and their principles applied. Accordingly, Christopher Columbus, with his three little vessels, sailed westward, to go to the east, and found an unknown continent. Others, like Cabot, Vespucci and Hudson, followed his course, and some dim knowledge was gained of this western land. It seems now as if it had been concealed from the world until the time should come

---

(1) Coffin's "Story of Liberty," p. 73.

(2) American Encyclopedia, Appleton, Vol. 13, p. 846, second column.

for the establishment of a new order in civil and religious government.

The THIRD GREAT STEP HAD BEEN TAKEN. A REFUGE FOR THE OPPRESSED OF EVERY CLIME HAD BEEN PROVIDED.

And now the world had come to the sixteenth century—a century crowded with events of the utmost importance to the human race. Time forbids more than a most rapid summary. Gutenberg's Bible had done its work. The learned knew it, and the time had come for them to use it. Then how those learned Bible students went trooping to the front to lead the advance! There, in the forefront, were Tyndale and Coverdale, Luther and Melancthon, Zwingle and Gustavus Vasa (1), Calvin and Knox, all born within the short space of twenty-six years, ending with the year 1509. The youngest was John Calvin, and next to him stood John Knox, and these two were the last to lay down their arms

---

(1) Gustavus Vasa is put in this list because, while in Lubeck for six months, he heard Luther preach, corresponded with him, and then, after he became King of Sweden, had the Lutheran adopted as the State Religion. He was instrumental in bringing over to Protestantism the Scandinavian countries. His grandson, Gustavus Adolphus—the Lion of the North—became the great Protestant Leader in the Thirty Years' War.

American Encyclopedia—Appleton, Vol. 8, p. 339, 2d column
American Encyclopedia—Appleton, Vol. 8, p. 340.

and report in person to their great Captain—the one in 1568 and the other in 1572—the great fight they had made.

The Bible was translated into English, into German, Helvetian, French, Swedish, Danish, Dutch, Italian, Spanish, Russian, Welsh, Hungarian, Icelandic, Polish and Bohemian (1), and edition after edition was printed and greedily sought after. Catechisms, Confessions of Faith, Rules of Discipline, Principles of Theology and Institutes of the Christian Religion were formulated, published and used. Congregations were gathered. Churches were built and sermons were preached daily, even to the hundreds of refugees who had fled from England to the safe haven in the Swiss Mountains (2).

The young were taught in schools and the more advanced in academies, where they were trained in theology and to preach the gospel (3). Systems of Church Government—one based "on the civil power of the Prince;" the other "on the republican basis of the congregation;"—the Lutheran and the Calvinistic—were introduced (4).

---
(1) Zell's Encyclopedia, Vol. 1, p 305.
(2) "Life of John Knox"—McCrie's Abridged, 1839, p. 80
(3) "The Protestant Revolution"—Seebohm, p. 198.
(4) "The Protestant Revolution"—Seebohm, p. 197 "Life of John Knox," p. 161.

Then through the Highlands and the Lowlands of Scotland went the ringing declaration of John Knox, "*who never feared the face of man:*" Rulers *must* govern according to laws the people have consented to, and, failing in this, they must be tried and punished, even with death if their crimes require it (1)—(a principle afterwards embodied in our Declaration of Independence).

And throughout those Highlands and Lowlands he established Congregations, Presbyteries, Synods, and, over all, a General Assembly, which first met in 1560, and in 1567 the Parliament made this republican form of Church Government—Presbyterian—the established Church of Scotland (2).

Meanwhile, that free lance among Kings—Henry VIII. of England—unable to longer use for his own selfish purposes the Roman Catholic Church he had served so well as to be called "Defender of the Faith," defied and cast off its supremacy, and had himself declared head of the Church in England. With the aid of able and learned men, its government, faith and form of worship were modified and

---

(1) "Life of John Knox"—McCrie's Abridged, pp. 148 and 218.

(2) "Life of John Knox"—McCrie's Abridged, p. 219.

reformed, and the Established Church of England took its place among the Protestant Churches of the world.

Meanwhile, too, a German army, composed mainly of Lutherans, at the call of the Emperor Charles V., crossed the Alps, joined the Spanish troops of the Emperor, and marched upon Rome. That city was taken and sacked, almost as the Goths and Vandals had sacked it a thousand years before. In contempt for the ecclesiastics, by whom they had been oppressed so long, the Germans stabled their horses in the church of St. Peter until it was full, and it was sure death for an ecclesiastic to appear on the streets unless disguised as a soldier (1).

Amid dire persecutions and slaughterings, the century drew to a close. But, "Rome had forever ceased to be the capital of Christendom" (2). "The principle of the old Roman civilization—the good of the few at the expense of the many"—had been exchanged for "Christian civilization, whose aim is to attain the highest good for the whole community" (3). To this civilization the nations of Teutonic

---

(1) "The Protestant Revolution"—Seebohm, pp. 154 and 155.
(2) "The Protestant Revolution"—Seebohm, pp. 154 and 155.
(3) "The Protestant Revolution"—Seebohm, p. 278.

origin—Germany, Switzerland, Denmark, Sweden, England, Scotland and the Netherlands—had given their adherence, while the nations of Latin origin " remained in allegiance to the Pope" (1).

The FOURTH GREAT STEP HAD BEEN IRRESISTIBLY TAKEN. A religion of the heart and conscience, based upon the Bible, had been established, and a foundation for republicanism in Church and State had been securely laid.

And how that work was consecrated! The blood of hundreds of thousands of men, women and children—infants even—burned at the stake and in furnaces, flayed alive, buried alive, impaled, torn to pieces on the racks of the Inquisition, killed in the heat of battle or butchered by frenzied cruelty, so consecrated it that freedom of religious thought can never " perish from off the earth."

Do you wonder that the people fled from such persecution? Do you wonder that, in the providence of God, this continent was held, undiscovered, until required as the place to which the persecuted could flee? And the persecuted for Christ's sake fled to it all through the seventeenth and a great part of the eighteenth centuries. They sailed over unknown

---

(1) " The Protestant Revolution"—Seebohm, p. 158.

waters, to unknown dangers, in an unknown world. They sailed from Switzerland, from France, from Germany, from the Netherlands, from Sweden, from England, from Scotland and from the north of Ireland, and they carried with them their Bibles, Catechisms and ideas of Church government. They settled along our sea-coast, from Maine to Georgia, and formed governments of themselves, for themselves and by themselves. Their ideas grew and expanded, and voluntarily blending themselves together, after the manner of the forceful commingling that made the Anglo-Saxons, they became strong and self-reliant, awaiting the fullness of time, when necessity should weld them into a new nation on the order of the Anglo-Saxons, with their language, their laws and their best characteristics.

But there was work yet to be done in the lands whence these people had fled, and it WAS done.

In 1603, James the Sixth, King of Scotland, became James the First, King of England. On Jan. 14, 1604, he "summoned the leading Puritan Ministers to meet him at Hampton Court, in the presence of the principal Bishops, in order that he might learn what ecclesiastical changes were desired by the Puritans" (1). Very little resulted from the conference beyond the action taken by the King, on a suggestion of Dr. Reynolds, of Oxford, who was considered "nearly, if not altogether, the most learned man in England" (2). That was the appointment of a large number of divines to revise the English translation of the Bible, and to publish an authorized version. The work began in 1606 and appeared in 1611. Of it a modern writer says:

"The simplicity, terseness and power of the Eng-
"lish version, to which the taste of England, after
"frequent wanderings, again and again returns as
"to its best classical model, we owe, and this should
"not be forgotten, to the poor, persecuted, but noble-
"minded, English reformer, William Tyndale, who
"in his English New Testament set a type which
"others in completing the whole Bible loyally fol-
"lowed."

Charles the First succeeded his father, James the First, in 1625. The Stuarts believed in the "divine right of Kings." They therefore insisted upon

---

(1) "The Puritan Revolution"—Gardiner, in "Epochs of Modern History," p. 12.

(2) "The Constitutional History of England"—Hallam. Vol. 1, p. 294, Note 3.

"The Westminster Assembly"—Mitchell, p. 69.

autocratic rule. Civil liberty had taken a strong hold upon the English people, and was growing. A friction, therefore, that became acute, occurred between King and Parliament. The necessities of the King rendered the assembling of Parliament necessary, and on Nov. 3, 1640, the Long Parliament met at Westminster (1). The struggle for supremacy began. There was a great desire for further religious reform, and, to appease it, the King, on Feb. 14, 1641, referred the reform of the government and liturgy of the Church to the wisdom of Parliament, which he desired " them to enter into speedily" (2).

By June 1, 1642, Parliament passed an act referring the subject to an assembly composed of Peers, Members of the Commons, and Divines, but the King would not approve it. A second and a third shared the same fate and then on June 12, 1643, it was passed as an ordinance not requiring the King's approval (3). It recited that Parliament had declared the Church Government to be evil and offensive and that such a government as

---

(1) "The Puritan Revolution"—Gardiner, in " Epochs of Modern History," p. 110.
(2) "The Westminster Assembly"—Mitchell, p. 107.
(3) "The Westminster Assembly,"—Mitchell, pp. 108 and 111.

may be "most agreeable to God's holy word and nearer agreement with the Church of Scotland and other reformed churches abroad" shall be settled, and empowered the assembly to confer upon such matters concerning the Liturgy, Discipline and Government of the Church of England or the doctrine of the same, as might be proposed by either House of Parliament (1). The assembly was to meet July 1, 1643 (2). About June 22, 1643, the King prohibited the meeting by proclamation (3). It met, however, at the time named and met nearly twelve hundred times thereafter, and of the members named for the Assembly, the records show that nine Peers, twenty-five members of the Commons, and one hundred and eight Divines were present at different times and composed the great Westminster Assembly. It reported a form of Church Government which never received the sanction of Parliament (4), though some portions of it were passed, in 1645, by the General Assembly of the Scottish Church and approved, but not ordained to be observed, by the Scottish Parliament.

(1) "The Westminster Assembly"—Mitchell, Ordinance, pp. IX and X.
(2) "The Westminster Assembly"—Mitchell, p. 128.
(3) "The Westminster Assembly"—Mitchell, p. 129.
(4) "The Westminster Assembly"—Mitchell, p. 264.

On Dec. 14, 1646, the Confession of Faith was finished and reported to Parliament, and again, on April 29, 1647, with Scripture proofs added. (1). With the exception of Chapters XXX. and XXXI., and portions of Chapters XX. and XXIV., it was approved by the Parliament.

The larger Catechism, substantially as it is now, was reported by the Assembly to Parliament on Oct. 22, 1647. It was never approved by Parliament, but it passed the Scottish General Assembly on July 20, 1648 (2).

The shorter Catechism, with proofs, was reported April 16, 1648; approved by both Houses of Parliament by Sept. 25, 1648; by the Scottish General Assembly on July 28, 1648, and, with the Larger Catechism, ratified by the Scottish Parliament on Feb. 7, 1649 (3).

That shorter Catechism, taken regularly, makes the young grow into strong men and women. It never loses its power, however bad the patient may grow. In the system once, it stays for life, and, though it may fail of a cure, still it checks the

---

(1) "The Westminster Assembly"—Mitchell, p. 367.
(2) "The Westminster Assembly"—Mitchell, p. 125.
(3) "The Westminster Assembly"—Mitchell, p. 139.

course of sin at every stage of the disease. Carlyle said of it:

"The older I grow—and I now stand upon the brink of eternity—the more comes back to me the first sentence in the Catechism, which I learned when a child, and the fuller and deeper its meaning becomes: What is the chief end of man? To glorify God and enjoy Him forever" (1).

THE FIFTH GREAT STEP HAD BEEN TAKEN. With a complete translation of the Bible, a Confession of Faith, a perfect Catechism, and a thoroughly-considered Form of Government submitted, Presbyterianism was ready for further advance.

The Haven of Refuge on this Continent, however, was in danger of being lost. A Latin race—the French—had numerous settlements on the St. Lawrence in Canada, a line of strong forts on the river and on the great lakes, Fort Duquesne in Pennsylvania, where Pittsburg is now, and strong positions on the New York lakes. They had made allies of the Indians, were ably commanded, and were extending their possessions down the Ohio and the Mississippi. They were warring with the Colonies, and the English Government was weak. England

---

(1) Quoted in "The Westminster Assembly"—Mitchell, p. 441.

was losing ground everywhere, when William Pitt —afterwards the great Earl of Chatham—said to the Duke of Devonshire: "My Lord, I am sure that I can save this country, and that nobody else can" (1). He was given "supreme direction of the war and of foreign affairs" (2). In 1758, he made a treaty with Frederick the Great, one item of which was the payment to Frederick of a subsidy of £670,000 a year (3). This was to enable Frederick the Great to keep the French forces engaged in Europe so that the English might gain control on this continent. The subsidy was paid for three years, and aggregated about $10,000,000. The colonial forces ably supported the English soldiers. Louisburg fell, then Ticonderoga, then Niagara and then Quebec. By 1760 "the whole province of Canada was subjugated" (4). The French retired, and, with this Continent preserved for the Anglo-Saxons, THE SIXTH GREAT STEP WAS TAKEN.

This brings us to Presbyterianism in this country. Mr. Justice Kennedy, of the Supreme Court

---

(1) "Macaulay's Essays," Vol. 2, p. 76.

(2) "Macaulay's Essays," Vol. 2, p. 75.

(3) "Frederick the Great"—Longman, in "Epochs of Modern History," p. 140.

(4) "Macaulay's Essays," Vol. 2, pp. 78 and 79.

of Pennsylvania, in an opinion filed in Presbyterian Congregation vs. Johnson, in May, 1841, and reported in 1st. Watts & Sergeant's Reports, pp. 51 and 52, gives the following short history of it:

"The first Presbyterian Church in the United
" States consisted of a single congregation, formed
" in the City of Philadelphia, about the year 1700,
" which is known now by the name of the First
" Presbyterian Church in that city. Increasing,
" however, in number and strength, several congre-
" gations were formed shortly afterwards. In 1704
" the first Presbytery was organized; and in 1716
" the first Synod consisting of four Presbyteries. It
" was called the Synod of Philadelphia; but in 1741
" a division took place, which gave rise to a second,
" called the Synod of New York. In 1758, however,
" these Synods became united again under the title
" of the Synod of New York and Philadelphia, and
" governed the Presbyterian Church in the United
" States until 1788, when the Presbyterians having
" increased greatly in number, and being dispersed
" over a great extent of territory, it was deemed
" expedient, in order to promote and preserve purity
" and prevent error from creeping into the Church,
" to increase the number of Synods, and to establish

"a General Assembly in imitation of that estab"lished by the Church of Scotland under the West"minster Confession of Faith, invested with execu"tive, legislative and judicial power over the whole
"church. The form of Government adopted by the
"Church of Scotland and given in Westminster
"Confession of Faith, was ever looked to by the
"Presbyterians in the United States as their guide
"and was followed and adopted by them, with the
"exception as to the power given to the Civil Mag"istrate in matters of religion, from time to time,
"as their numbers increased and rendered it expe"dient, if not necessary, to do so. They began first
"by forming themselves into a single congregation;
"next into a Presbytery, as soon as the requisite
"number of congregations were formed to compose
"it. Then, as the number of Presbyteries was in"creased, a Synod was organized; after that several
"particular Synods and ultimately the General As"sembly, or what in other words may be called the
"National Synod."

It is generally conceded, however, that Presbyterianism had an earlier date in the United States than Judge Kennedy assigned to it.

The Rev. J. E. Rockwell in 1854 wrote:

"About the year 1690, Francis Makemie, from "the north of Ireland, and John Hampton, from "Scotland, who were laboring as Missionaries on "behalf of a Society in London, succeeded in organ-"izing Churches after the Scottish model in the "eastern part of Maryland. A company of Scotch "emigrants also were organized as a Church at the "same time, who came in a body to this country "with their pastor, Rev. Nathaniel Taylor, and set-"tled in Upper Marlborough.

"The Churches of Snowhill, Rehoboth, Monokin "and Wicomico were formed by Mr. Makemie, "whose name and memory are still cherished as an "able and devoted servant and minister of Christ.

"In 1698, the first Presbyterian Church of Phil-"adelphia was formed by a number of English, "Welsh and French Protestants, who united under "the pastoral care of Rev. Mr. Andrews, of Boston" (1).

Gabriel Thomas, who came in 1681, on the first ship that was bound from England for this country after it was called Pennsylvania, and who lived here for fifteen years, wrote, in 1697, "An Historical and

---

(1) "Sketches of the Presbyterian Church"—Rockwell, p. 225.

"Geographical Account of the Province and Coun-
"try of Pennsylvania and of West New Jersey
"in America," which was published in London in
1698. He says: "But it remained with very little
"improvement till the year 1681, in which William
"Penn, Esq., had the country given him by King
"Charles the Second. * * * Since that time
"the industrious (nay indefatigable) inhabitants
"have built a noble and beautiful city, and called it
"Philadelphia, which contains above two thousand
"houses, all inhabited, and most of them stately and
"of brick, generally three stories high, after the
"mode in London, and as many as several families
"in each (1).

"They pay no tithes, and their taxes are incon-
"siderable; the place is free for all persuasions in
"a sober and civil way; for the Church of England
"and the Quakers bear equal share in the govern-
"ment; they live friendly and well together; there
"is no persecution for religion, nor ever likely to
"be" (2).

"The way of Worship the Swedes use in this
"Country, is the Lutheran; the English have four

---

(1) "Thomas's Pennsylvania and New Jersey, 1698," pp. 4 and 5.
(2) Idem, pp 35 and 36.

"sorts of Assemblies or Religious Meetings here; "as first, the Church of England, who built a very "fine church in the City of Philadelphia in the "year 1695; secondly, the Ana-Baptists; thirdly, "the Presbyterians, and two sorts of Quakers" (1).

Speaking of the Quaker George Keith's writings and sayings, he says:

"And he tells the Presbyterian Minister that he "must go to the Pope of Rome for his call, for he "had not Scripture for it," and he adds: "this was "in the year 1693 in Pensilvania." And again, he says: "and his letter also in Mary Land against the Presbyterian Catechism, Printed at Boston in New England in 1695" (2).

This is newly discovered evidence of the early existence of Presbyterianism in this country and proves that it existed here considerably over two hundred years ago. It grew rapidly and, as stated by Justice Kennedy, its Church affairs were ruled over by the Synod of Philadelphia at first, afterwards of New York and Philadelphia, until after the Revolution and down to 1788. It was the only Church in the country, prior to the Revolution,

---
(1) Idem, pp. 51 and 52.
(2) Idem, pp. 52-3 and 4.

whose affairs were so ruled over by a Legislative and Judicial body, composed of Ministers and Elders, from Georgia to New England, annually chosen by the people they represented, and they were imbued with the spirit of liberty and in favor of a republican form of government in civil affairs, such as they had in their own Church. The churches of the Congregationalists and the Baptists were separate and distinct units. The churches of England were controlled by the parent Church in England (1). The Methodists had no class, as it is termed, or congregation in this country until 1766, and their first Conference was held in 1773 (2). The Reformed Dutch Church was restricted in its limits, had no English preaching until 1763, and was without a Church Judicatory until 1771 (3). The German Reformed Church was governed from Holland until 1793 (4). The Catholics then were insignificant in numbers, and the Quakers were non-combatants. It is apparent, therefore, that the Presbyterian Church was the only Church in this country, prior

---

(1) " Westminster Anniversary Addresses, 1898," pp.336-7-8.
(2) "New American Encyclopedia"—Appleton, Vol. 11, p.464.
(3) "New American Encyclopedia"—Appleton, Vol. 14, pp. 256 and 6.
(4) "New American Encyclopedia"—Appleton, Vol. 14, p.258

to the Revolution, governed by a representative body—a body that had then existed for sixty years, from 1716 to 1776. It would be interesting to trace the influence of those representatives in moulding opinion, and directing it towards free government, culminating in the Declaration of Independence in 1776. Time, however, forbids. Certain it is, that their influence controlled. It was the vote of a Presbyterian—a lawyer from our own town—James Wilson—that gave a bare majority in the vote of the Pennsylvania Delegation cast for the Declaration of Independence (1). It was Dr. John Witherspoon, a lineal descendant of John Knox, President of Princeton College, and head of its Presbyterian School of Divinity, who declared in Congress "that in his judgment the country was not only ripe for Independence, but was in danger of becoming rotten for want of it, if its Declaration were longer delayed" (2). It was not delayed, and its assertion that Governments derive their just powers from the

---

(1) "History of Cumberland and Adams Counties," p. 87. "History of the United States" - Bancroft Centenary Ed., Vol. 5, p. 320. "First Presbyterian Church. Carlisle"—Wing. p. 93.

(2) "History of the United States"—Bancroft, Centenary Ed., Vol. 5, p. 318.

consent of the governed was made good when a treaty of peace with Great Britain was ratified in 1783.

Then came the formation of a National Constitution, to bind the States together under one Government, deriving its powers from the consent of the governed. Time again forbids tracing Presbyterian influence in its accomplishment. Suffice it to say, that Madison, called the father of the Constitution, although an Episcopalian, received his education under Dr. John Witherspoon, the head of the Presbyterian College at Princeton (1), that James Wilson, the Presbyterian lawyer, formerly of Carlisle, was on the committee that reported the Constitution to the Convention, and he secured its adoption by Pennsylvania (2), and that Gouverneur Morris, then of Pennsylvania, who corrected and arranged the final draft of it, was a lineal descendant of an officer of Oliver Cromwell's army (3). That Constitution, on June 21, 1788, was ratified by

---

(1) "Appleton's Cyclopedia of American Biography," Vol. J, p. 165.

(2) "History of the Constitution of the United States"—Bancroft, pp. 274 and 384.

(3) "Appleton's Cyclopedia of American Biography," Vol. 4, pp. 414 and 415.

the required number of States (1), and became the fundamental law of the land.

In keeping with this advance to Civil Liberty in our form of Government, the Presbyterian Church in the United States went forward to *its* larger development in the same direction. Beginning in 1786, the work was completed in May, 1788, by the adoption of the Report of the Committee in favor of a General Assembly, similar to that of the Church of Scotland, the Westminster Confession of Faith, with all mixture of civil with Church matters eliminated therefrom, the Directory for Worship and the Catechisms (2). At the head of the committee was Dr. John Witherspoon, and a member of it was a Presbyterian minister—Dr. George Duffield—who had been for some years pastor of the Church in Carlisle—and to whose congregation James Wilson, the signer of the Declaration of Independence, and one of the framers of the Constitution of the United States, belonged (3). These Constitutions, in Civil

---

(1) "Appleton's Cyclopedia of American Biography."

(2) "Sketches of the Presbyterian Church"—Rockwell, 1854. p. 740.

(3) "Sketches of the Presbyterian Church"—Rockwell, p. 240. The American Cyclopedia—Appleton, Vol. 13, p. 813.

Appleton's Cyclopedia of American Biography, Vol. 2, p. 248.

and in Church affairs, were adopted by the respective powers here in our own State of Pennsylvania.

The first Congress of the United States met on March 4, 1789. The first General Assembly of the Presbyterian Church in the United States met on the third Thursday in May, 1789.

THE SEVENTH GREAT STEP HAD BEEN TAKEN. A Republican form of Government in Civil and in Church affairs, entirely separate and distinct from each other, had been put in operation in a land set apart for freedom.

The unit in the State is the Township or Town. In the Church it is the congregation. A number of townships and towns form the County. A number of churches form the Presbytery. A number of Counties make the State. A number of Presbyteries constitute the Synod. The States make the General Government. The Presbyteries through the Synods make the General Assembly. State and Church alike derive all power from the governed, whose consent is required to change the fundamental law. Each has its own sphere and conflicts not with the other—in fact they harmonize. Thus Chief Justice Tilghman, of Pennsylvania, in Riddle vs. Stevens, a Presbyterian

Church case, decided in 1816, and reported in 2nd Sergeant & Rawle's Reports, says on page 543:

"Every Church has a discipline of its own. It is "necessary that it should be so, because, without "rules and discipline, no body composed of nu-"merous individuals can be governed. But this "discipline is confined to spiritual affairs. It oper-"ates on the mind and conscience, without pretend-"ing to temporal authority. No member of the "Church can be fined or imprisoned. But be he "minister or layman he may be admonished, re-"proved and finally ejected from the Society. So "he may retire from the Society at his own free "will. Under these restrictions religious discipline "may produce much good, without infringing on "civil liberty."

From 1789 on each has advanced side by side until to-day the population of the country is 70,-000,000, while the Presbyterian Church and its Calvinistic Allies, with their constituencies, amount to one-ninth or more of the entire people—a larger proportion than that possessed by any other church in the country.

It remained to demonstrate that a Republican form of Civil Government was strong. It resisted foes from without. Could it overcome foes within itself? The war of the Rebellion tried it. Terrible as it was the State emerged from it purified from slavery and with a strength that astonished the world. There the parallel ends. In the State the individual is subject to the will of the majority, while in the Church the conscience of the individual controls membership.

From our present standpoint, looking backward over the course of events, it would seem, therefore, that there has been a steady unfolding of some great plan for the human race. Each movement led to a definite result not intended by the actors in it. All thus far have culminated in establishing in a country, unknown before, civil and religious liberty based upon personal responsibility of the individual to the laws of the majority on the one side, and on the other, to the laws of the Creator as made known in the Bible. The movement originated in a nation which resulted from the commingling of various races and its continuation is in a nation produced by a commingling thus far of a much greater number of human races. It was caused by a growing knowledge of the Bible, an absolute belief in its teachings and an indestructible faith in its promises.

Surely it has been, and is, part of some great plan working out under divine direction, and it behooves each individual to work for, and not against, that plan.

This church is one of the professedly working units. It is a member of the leading Presbyterian body in the world. Has it been working for, or against, the Lord's plan? It has lived thus far sixty-six years. Take a rapid survey of what the years disclose, and then answer the question for yourselves.

The Rev. George Duffield was the pastor of the Presbyterian congregation in Carlisle when, early in 1832, he published a large volume entitled "Spiritual Life, &c" (1). Dr. Wing artlessly says:

"He had, in his congregation, a number of per-
"sons who were capable of appreciating theological
"statements, and whose minds were not satisfied
"with his explanations. They were ardently at-
"tached to those views which he so zealously as-
"sailed as injurious to souls." (2) From these "persons who were capable of appreciating theological statements," a petition was presented by Mr. An-

---

(1. The First Presbyterian Church of Carlisle—Wing, p. 180.
(2) The First Presbyterian Church of Carlisle—Wing, p. 182.

HISTORICAL ADDRESS. 91

drew Blair on Nov. 28th, 1832, to the Carlisle Presbytery which then met at Newville in this county, asking to be formed into a separate society, under the care of the Presbytery, from and after January 1st, 1833 (1).

The Presbytery, by a unanimous vote, granted the prayer of the petitioners, and appointed a committee of two ministers to organize the present Church. That committee met with the petitioners on Saturday, the 12th day of January, 1833, in the County Hall, at Carlisle, and organized the Church. One of the committee was the father of the present senior Senator from Pennsylvania—Mr. Quay—and one of the petitioners to be organized into a Church was the grandfather of the present junior Senator from Pennsylvania—Mr. Penrose. The petitioners were 77 in number—65 communicants and 12 non-communicant pew-holders. Of the communicants, three were Elders, four were Deacons, and eight were Trustees—a majority of the Board of the Old Church. All of the four Deacons were also Trustees, and are included in the eight. The three Elders were Robert Clark, ordained in October, 1816; (2)

---
(1) Record of Sessions, Second Presbyterian Church, Carlisle, Pa.," p. 1.
(2) "First Presbyterian Church, of Carlisle"—Wing, p. 154.

John McClure and Andrew Blair, ordained Dec. 25, 1825 (2). At the meeting for organization, Mr. Quay preached the sermon from Verse 7 of Psalm 62—" My refuge is in God." It might be well for his talented son, the Senator, about this time, to look up that sermon and study it.

The organization was effected by the election of Andrew Blair, John McClure and Robert Clark to be Ruling Elders, and Peter B. Smith, Robert Irvine, John Proctor and Robert Giffen to be Deacons—all having held the same offices in the Old Church.

At the meeting three committees were appointed —one of five members, including Charles B. Penrose and George Metzger, neither of whom was a communicant, to procure a charter; one of twelve members, " to superintend the financial affairs of the congregation for one year, or until a charter be procured, if that be obtained within the year;" and one of fifteen members, " to procure subscriptions * * * for the purpose of aiding us in purchasing a lot of ground and erecting a suitable house of worship," with authority " to purchase a suitable site for said building." It was resolved also that

---

(2) " **First Presbyterian Church, of Carlisle**"—Wing, p. 166.

there should be public worship of and preaching to the congregation every Sabbath, and Rev. Daniel McKinley was invited to preach on the Sabbaths not provided for by the Presbytery. *The congregation had begun its life as a member of the greatest Presbyterian body in the world.*

The old congregation had a fund of twenty-five hundred dollars remaining from the sale and conveyance, on January 30, 1827, by deed recorded in the Recorder's Office of Cumberland County, in Record Book "KK," Vol. 1, page 163, to Philip Weaver, of the Globe farm, at Meeting House Springs, of 143 acres 85½ perches, for $3,500. At a congregational meeting held in that Church, after Presbytery had taken action upon the petition for a separate church organization, it was ordered that this twenty-five hundred dollars be turned over to the new Church, and on December 17, 1832, the Board of Trustees, under the action of the congregation, directed that sum to be paid to Robert Clark and Andrew Blair, in trust "for the congregation to be set off, to enable them to build a house of worship" (1).

---

(1) "First Presbyterian Church, of Carlisle"—Wing, p. 189.
 Corrected by Rev Dr. J. A. Murray, in "Carlisle Volunteer," of January 10, 1878.

The committee to purchase a suitable site, on April 1, 1833, took a conveyance, recorded in the Recorder's Office, in Book "OO," Vol. 1, page 252, from Alexander Oliver to John Hays, Charles B. Penrose, George A. Lyon, James Thompson and John Agnew, for and in behalf of the Second Presbyterian Church, of Carlisle, of the lot on the southeast corner of Hanover and Pomfret streets, in Carlisle, of 63 feet in front on Hanover street, and 160 feet 5 inches on Pomfret street, for the consideration of $2,200. The grantees in this deed, by Deed Poll of September 16, 1839, recorded in the Recorder's Office, in Record Book "WW," Vol. 1, page 223, conveyed this lot to the Church corporation. Later on the Church sold a portion of it fronting on Pomfret street, and subsequently re-purchased it.

John C. Trautwine, Esq., was employed to prepare plans for the church building, and a Mr. Holman was given the contract for its erection. Time has not permitted the ascertainment of its cost, but on April 7, 1834, it was estimated that a sum not exceeding $1,400 would pay in full any balance to be paid on the contract, as well as the furnishing of the Church. By May 3, 1834, subscriptions for the purpose, amounting to $1,461.50, were reported (1). Mr. Trautwine would accept no compensation for his services, and on September 29, 1834, it was ordered that a silver cup, of the value of thirty dollars, with a suitable inscription, "be presented to him, with thanks, for the elegant plan of a church edifice." At the same time it was ordered that Mr. Holman, the contractor, be informed " of the entire satisfaction and gratification * * * in the construction and completion of the Church edifice. *The lot had been purchased, and the Church had been built and paid for.*

The committee appointed for the purpose obtained a charter of incorporation, which was approved by the Governor on April 8, 1833, and is to be found in " Laws of the General Assembly of the State of Pennsylvania" for 1832-3, page 302. The full corporate name is "The Second Presbyterian Church, in the Borough of Carlisle and County of Cumberland." Fifteen incorporators are named in the Act, in the following order: Peter B. Smith, John Proctor, John Huston, C. B. Penrose, G. Metzger, Esq., James Hamilton, Esq., Alexander Gregg, Robert Irvine, John Stuart, John Williamson, Esq., George

(1) Minutes, pp. 13 and 14.

A. Lyon, Esq., Robert Giffen, Andrew Holmes. Abraham Lamberton, John Hays; five of whom were lawyers, and four, including three of the lawyers, were non-communicants. They met on April 12, 1833, at the house of George A. Lyon, Esq.,—the stone house now of Mr. William Barnitz, on the north side of East Main street—and organized by the election of George A. Lyon, Esq., as President, James Hamilton, Esq., as Secretary, and William Irvine, Esq., as Treasurer (1).

The corporation had come into life.

On June 5th, 1833, the congregation, by a unanimous vote, elected the Rev. Daniel McKinley as Pastor, and on Aug. 7th, 1833, at two o'clock p. m.. the Presbytery met with the congregation in the College Chapel, and duly installed him.

Thus the congregation was duly organized, with Pastor, Elders and Deacons, with a charter of incorporation, and an organized Board of Trustees, with a Church property of its own and paid for, and it was ready to proceed on its career after "Glory and Happiness."

The charter of the church provides: "That all "elections to be held in pursuance of this Act shall

---
(1) Minutes, p. 3.

"be by ballot * * * that no persons shall be
" entitled to vote at said elections, nor shall any one
" be elected as trustee, who is not a stated worship-
" per in said congregation, and whose name has not
" been entered on the books of the congregation at
" least one year immediately preceding any of said
" elections as a contributor to said Church in a sum
" not less than one dollar and fifty cents, and who
" shall be in arrears for such or any part thereof for
" the space of thirty days; * * * that the
" Pastor of said Congregation and ruling Elders shall
" not hold any other office, and said Pastor shall be
" disqualified from the right of voting." A committee, consisting of Charles B. Penrose, Peter B. Smith and George A. Lyon, appointed April 12, 1833, reported By-Laws for the corporation on June 3rd, 1833, which were unanimously approved by the Board, and, on June 5, 1833, unanimously adopted by the congregation (1). The charter qualifications of electors were incorporated in By-Law No. 5.

These provisions separated the charter of this Church from all other church charters that have

---
(1) Minutes, p. 7.

been examined, and absolutely cut off the spiritual matters and officers of the congregation from its temporal affairs and their management. That there might be no mistake as to their effect the session of the church on Nov. 21st, 1835, addressed a very carefully prepared overture to the congregation asking "that By-Law No. 5 be altered so as to "restrict its operation to elections for Pastor and "Trustees, and to questions which relate to the "pecuniary affairs of the congregation, "and "that "in all elections for Elders or Deacons, no person "shall be entitled to vote who is not a member of "the church in full communion, over the age of "twenty-one years, and who does not contribute "his just proportion according to his own engage- "ments or the rules of the congregation to all its "necessary or benevolent expenses." The congregation on Dec. 3rd, 1835, in response to the overture, made the changes requested (1).

Thus again and finally the line was drawn between the temporal and spiritual affairs of the congregation. The larger body—the Corporation—including communicants and non-communicants—

---

(1) **Minutes of Session, p 17.**
   Minutes of Trustees, p. 27.

has exclusive control over temporal matters and the election of Pastors and Trustees, while the smaller body of communicants has just as exclusive control over spiritual affairs through its representative—the Session. It is a smaller body within a larger one—like a State within the Union—each having its separate and distinct powers and neither interfering with the other. It thus becomes apparent that a Presbyterian Constituency exists and is composed of non-communicants who are stated worshippers in and contributors to the Church. It makes these non-communicants members of the Church in the larger sense of the term and gives them a voice in the selection of Pastors and in the business management of the Church. It adds to the Church a strong element, and these constituents, from themselves and their families, furnish recruits to the ranks of the communicants. In this the Presbyterian Church stands almost, if not entirely, alone among the churches of this country.

Over the Church thus constituted, its chosen Session ruled. In length of services as an Elder, Mr. Robert Clark led. He was ordained in October, 1816, and died in January, 1856, having served in the First Church seventeen years, and in this Church twenty-two years, in all somewhat over thirty-nine years. Mr. Andrew Blair was ordained on Dec. 25, 1825, served the First Church seven years, and this Church twenty-eight and a half years to his death, in July, 1861, in all thirty-five and a half years. His service to this Church was the longest. Mr. John McClure was a brother-in-law of Mr. Andrew Blair, was ordained at the same time with him, and served the First Church for the same period. He last appeared at a meeting of the Session Aug. 19, 1839, resigned as its Clerk, because of continued ill-health, September 10, 1840, and died in April, 1841, having practically served this Church six years and a half, which made an aggregate service as an Elder of thirteen and a half years. These gentlemen ruled as if they had ever before them the Declaration, found in the 8th section of the 1st Chapter of "The Form of Government" of the Presbyterian Church in the United States, as follows : "*The vigour and strictness of its discipline will contribute to the glory and happiness of any Church*"—and which deserves to be written in letters of gold upon the walls of every Church. They divided the territory within their jurisdiction, and assigned one of their number to each district, so that the members of the Church could be regularly visited. In this way, and with Pastoral visits, the members of the Session became familiar with the conduct of every member of the Church, and if it did not accord with what they interpreted the standard of Christian behavior to be, they unhesitatingly, but with the utmost kindness, advised, reproved, and, if necessary, summoned before them and dealt with the party according to the rules of the Church. They set their faces like flint against theatre going, balls and dancing parties, even attendance at the latter, and against every species of fashionable amusement, and through their Pastor, made a deliverance on the subject, which was heartily approved by the Presbytery. From time to time other members were added to the Session, and one by one dropped out again, but the ruling continued the same through the pastorates of Mr. McKinley, Mr. McGill, Mr. Moore. Mr. Lillie, Mr. Johnston and Mr. Eells, down to the death of Mr. Blair, because Mr. Blair dominated the Session and the Pastors.

Tall and massive in frame, with a big square head, well set on his broad shoulders, he was stalwart in mind and body. Of a Scotch family, which for two generations before him resided here, he was imbued with all the Scotch reverence for religion, and with all the Scotch intolerance of sin. Utterly fearless, he denounced in scathing terms every form of sin, but with a glowing smile that lighted up all his rugged features he was ever ready to welcome the repentant sinner. He was a close student of the Bible, and, thoroughly conversant with the doctrines and government of the Church, he ruled his own life by them. For many years, and until his death, he was the Superintendent of the Sabbath-school, and he regularly conducted the Friday evening prayer-meeting. Until a few years before his death the "Thunders of Sinai" seemed to be sounding in his ears, and he passed them on to all the sinners around him, then those thunders almost entirely ceased to sound for him, and the quiet peace of perfect love seemed to pervade his whole being. This was most apparent when the great religious wave of 1857 and 1858 passed over the country. Everywhere noonday prayer-meetings were held and joined in by all Protestant denominations. They were held in this town in a room in Marion Hall, and in his addresses and prayers in those meetings Mr. Blair was happier, more eloquent and more effective than he had ever been; and the main-spring of it all was the intense overflowing love that sounded in his words and shone upon his countenance. Shortly thereafter he was in the grasp of disease. Then, slowly and painfully, but serenely, that "grand old man" went down to his grave and up to his Lord.

Mr. Robert Clark was a shorter man than Mr. Blair, broad, heavy shouldered and with a large head. His whole person indicated unyielding determination. He, too, was of Scotch descent, and his Presbyterianism was ingrained. Living some miles out in the country, no one was more constant in church attendance and at the meetings of Session. He was willing and ready to go anywhere and do anything in the line of his duty. He was kind, warmhearted, but strict and positive in his views. Of rather a retiring disposition, he shunned, but never shirked, public leadership. His high sense of duty made him obedient to its calls and he responded to every demand made upon him. He stood side by side with Mr. Blair. With him he was the friend and confidant of his Pastors and with him he ruled wisely and well.

Another of those old time worthies was Mr. James Hamilton, who lived and worked in this Church for forty years, until he too joined the great majority, in

January, 1873. Almost painfully deficient in self-confidence, although morally brave, he could never be induced to be ordained as a Ruling Elder, to which office he was three times chosen. He was peculiar in many ways, but never so when it was a matter of Church work, and in his own modest, retiring way he did as much as any Ruling Elder could ever hope to do. He was slow in forming a conclusion but when once formed there was an end of the matter. He too was a Bible student and a thorough Presbyterian. For many years he had a Bible class for young ladies in Sabbath-school, and after the death of Mr. Blair became Superintendent of the School until early in 1869 he suggested that the Superintendent should be annually appointed, and in that way he was enabled to retire. He took great personal interest in the young who came under his teaching—made parties for them at his house or took them on picnics to one of his farms. On the inner side of his office door were written the names of his young lady scholars and the years of their scholarship, so that at the time he died there must have been over two hundred names there. To each one he gave some little token of regard—a Bible or a hymn book, a Confession of Faith or some other book, and in each was written over his signature some words of admonition or of Scripture. Now, many of those young ladies are wives and mothers and grandmothers scattered all over the United States, but wherever they are they have a kindly feeling for peculiar, genial and warm hearted Mr. Hamilton, and are instilling, into the minds of children and grandchildren, the words of wisdom he taught, so that they too may become living monuments of his work on earth.

How memories of those old worthies come thronging upon us! These few are but types of the others. They were forceful, strong minded, positive men and women, and they laid the foundation of this Church deep and strong. They passed it on to their successors, and when in time, after the pastorate of Mr. Bliss, it came to be placed under a pastorate that has now seen thirty years of life, it had become so great that it could afford to expend, for a parsonage and for this larger place of worship that its needs required, nearly sixty thousand dollars. During those thirty years the work has been carried forward and upward, and looking back over the sixty-six years that have passed since that little knot of men and women were formed into a Presbyterian Congregation, we can see, all along the years, the potential influence its men and women exercised in this community and in this county. It has been an influence exceeding any other, and it sprang from the lives and the character of the members of this Congregation. For almost sixty years the President Judges of your Courts have been of your number or have owed their appointment, nomination and election to their families or their friends among you. So long as Associate Judges sat upon the Bench, almost without exception, a Second Presbyterian was one of them. A long line of eminent lawyers, beginning with Metzger and Penrose and ending with Sharpe, added ability and force, while, through Banks officered and controlled by your people, the financial affairs of the County have been ruled. Good old Presbyterian ladies, among you, originated the Ladies' Benevolent Aid Society, that has done and is doing such good work among the poor of the town. Missionaries in foreign lands, Ministers of the Gospel, prominent men and rising young men, everywhere, have gone out from you, and the teaching and the training they received here are helping to better the world.

What has been done in the past can be done in

the years that the future contains, and, under the leadership of your *thirty-year* old Pastor, the work can be so advanced and increased that your successors can look back with greater pride than you do, and can see how this Church has worked in harmony with the divine plan, in the establishment of civil and religious liberty upon this continent, as shown in our form of Government and in the Presbyterian Church.

ADDRESSES.

Sabbath Evening, January 1, 1899.

REV. WILLIAM A. WEST,
President of Metzger College, Carlisle,
Presiding.

President West expressed his high appreciation of the honor conferred upon him by the invitation to preside at a service which would help to mark an occasion so interesting and memorable as this anniversary. He referred in feeling terms to the very close relations which he sustained alike to this pastor and people, and having spoken of the honorable record which had been made by many of the pastors in the Presbytery of Carlisle as to the matter of long periods of service, he introduced the first speaker of the evening, Dr. Crawford, as one who had helped to install the pastor of this Church thirty years ago, having given him, at that time, by appointment of Presbytery, the solemn and official charge of fidelity to his trust in the sight of God.

"THE MINISTRY, THE GLORY OF CHRIST."

BY

REV. J. AGNEW CRAWFORD, D. D.

"Our brethren * * are the glory of Christ"—II Cor. viii. 23.

There is a mellow light that lingers yet on ancient Greece, and a winsome charm in that classic land, not less for the Christian than for the unbelieving scholar. Our religion has hallowed much of its soil, and of its water-ways as well. It has made Athens and Achaia, and Philippi, and Corinth, and Cenchrea, the Ægean and the Cyclades, immortal for us all, and not less so the narrow Isthmus which joins Greece proper to the Peloponnesus, and upon which the city of Corinth sat like a queen. It was said of it, that it was in a military point of view the eye of Greece, as Athens was intellectually. Yet no moral soil could have been less promising for the planting of the truth of God. For Corinth was so unclean and so voluptuous that " to Corinthianize" meant to be utterly bad. Yet a Christian Church was founded there, to which the Apostle Paul sent two of his most important Epistles. Titus the Evangelist by his request was making a visit to the Church there, accompanied by several of the brethren. And writing to the Corinthians, Paul says, " If any make inquiry in regard to these ministers, they are the messengers of the Churches and the glory of Christ." It is to this clause I now draw your attention, " *Our brethren are the glory of Christ.*"

Our friend, and associate in the ministry, your worthy pastor, is one of these. He has served this church for thirty years standing all this time at his post sentinel, counsellor, teacher, pastor, bishop, friend, and we are here to-night to congratulate him on the good Providence of God which has thus ordered, and upon important work done here for the Master. He has taught, and warned men, seeking " to present them at last perfect in Christ Jesus." He has cried aloud of the coming doom, and pointed to the refuge, and urged men to run to it. He has been in charge of your high spiritual affairs, giving you the best of his brain and heart, of his time, of his acquisitions, of his ripest years. It cannot all have been in vain,—nay rather may we not believe you will be his crown on the coronation day.

Let me call your attention to this remarkable

phrase of Paul, "Our brethren—the glory of Christ," The common explanation of it is that "the ministry is an honor to the Gospel, and are greatly instrumental in promoting the glory of the Saviour"—that they are the glory of Christ just as all Christians are, in this that they aim to honor Him by their holy living, by their diligence and success in duty, and by their love and loyalty to Him.

But I cannot think that this account of these remarkable words exhausts their meaning. They make a special statement not in regard to the Church at large, but the ministry. Whatever the words mean, they affirm it of the men whom the Son of God has sent to preach His Gospel, and I do not find that they are used either of the Old Testament levites or prophets, or priests—but of the Christian ministry. We are speaking now not of the men, but of the order taken as a distinct and separate class, and the assertion is that "*they are the glory of Christ.*"

I. In this that they make actual in fact, and historically for all time the Saviour's own ideal of the way in which the world must be reached by His Gospel.

There are other ways conceivable by us in which

He could have reached His end. He might, for example, have sent the seraphs who would gladly and with swiftest feet have run on such an errandry. Or He might have ordered an inspired commission to sit in the city of Jerusalem through the years, to whom from far and near men might have come to learn the truth; or He might have put forth a secret influence on the minds of men by His Holy Spirit so that they could have been saved.

But of all the possibilities that were present to His mind to secure His end, Jesus fixed upon this of the human ministry, and certainly for some sufficient reason. It is remarkable that He limited Himself to this, and that He gave no leave to His Church to adopt any other plan, whatever her condition might at any juncture or crisis seem to demand. He would risk all—if I may so put it—on this. Then He disappeared, going away to the sky, and having in fact said to the apostles—I leave in your hands this great affair; I depend upon you; my commission to you is beyond recall; this lost world must be reached even to the last man before I can return to close the affairs of My Kingdom here and to settle the destinies of all men. You may not lean on any human arm, nor make any league with earthly kingdoms to secure your success. "I will give you a mouth and wisdom, which all your adversaries shall not be able to gainsay nor resist," and you shall receive such an enduement of power as shall make you equal to your great task, and men shall know Me through you. Nothing like this, nothing approaching this, was ever said to any but to the apostles, and so through them to the line of the "Ministry of Reconciliation," as Paul calls them.

Now, for men, mere men, to stand in any such relation to the Son of God as this, to have Him falling back, if I may so say, on them, the Infinite upon the finite, this is indeed for them to be "the glory of Christ." One would think that man could hardly be pushed to such prominence, even with God behind him. How can anything so dark, so limp, so much in disarray as even sanctified manhood is, be relied upon for a task so "huge"* as this? If you lift the ministry into a priesthood—if that would even be lifting it—or if you sink it into a mere association of good men, who with no authority but simply fired with zeal go out to reclaim and save this wandering and fractured humanity of ours, you have shorn it of its strengh, and made it other than

---
* The adjective is Archbishop Leighton's.

the Lord Jesus made it. It is doubtful if it could do the work to be done, and whether it would indeed realize the Saviour's ideal.

II. The Christian ministry is the glory of Christ in that they serve in this which is His own Economy, and carry a special commission from Him so to do.

In this very Epistle, and in that to the Hebrews as well, Paul argues the temporary character of the former dispensation, giving the reasons why it could not continue: "It waxed old;" it was cut constantly by the tooth of Time. It made nothing perfect. It could not purify the conscience of any worshipper. It was the ministration of condemnation. Outwardly it was decked and fair. The pattern of it all was shown to Moses on the Mount. There was blue, and purple and scarlet fine-twined linen. The cloud of fragrant incense was ever going up, and through the years the ground round about the altars was red and wet with the blood of sacrifice. If any religion whose glory lay in externals bade fair to stand, it was that old Economy. But it did not. It could not. It was not in vain. To say that would be to reflect upon God himself. It did not die before its time, and it was no dishonor for it to die then. It is no shame to the ephemera that they dance in the sun for a day only, and that they have no yesterday and no to-morrow. The things which God has made, and which touch their goal, may not be rated low. And so the Mosaic system is to be reverently conceived of, for it fulfilled its mission. But the kingdom of the Son of God rose upon its ruins, never to know decline.

> "Deem not the irrevocable past
> As wholly wasted, wholly vain,
> If rising on its wrecks at last
> To something nobler we attain."

For He Himself whose are the everlasting years is its base, and corner stone, and cap-stone as well. His is this new era which nearly two thousand years ago dawned upon our globe, and the Christianity which shines now in its splendor, original as it is, and radiant with spiritual beauty as it is, is His. It is the working out of His own divine thought, the product at once of His wisdom and of His mighty power. The mystic force which is so plainly in it, and before which nothing that was in its way has been able to stand, all tells of Him. It has all the elements of a world's religion. In its author there was nothing narrow nor limited. Jew though He was, He had no distinguishing marks of the men of His nation. Nothing was more remarkable as a feature of His divine-human character than its universality. He was not representative of any class or nation. He was not oriental in any peculiar way in His teaching. Indeed, He drew all men to Him, and all this was His glory in view of the errand which brought Him here. His thought embraced humanity. He stood central amid the universal wreck to rescue, to lift up, to build into the dark interstices which men call ruins, to restore that which He took not away.

This present Economy of Grace is His in a very special and real way. Jesus, says the apostle, is the author of our faith. And in this the Christian ministry is appointed to serve. And that, not in any merely tentative way or as an experiment, and as being one of several agencies that might have been tested, but as the one and only agency preferred by the Lord Himself, and relied upon by Him for reaching the whole world with His salvation. And for this purpose they carry His personal commission, and so they are indeed His glory, as our verse declares. Back of them is He, the authority that sends, and sanctions, and supports. Our Church refuses the notion of what is called the "Apostolical Succession," as that phrase is usually explained.

At the same time it is certain that in all the past there has been a plurality of Presbyters who have been the historic channels through which the ministerial power and authority have come. If the chain which unites the ministry to the Lord Jesus be broken in fact, so that we are historically cut off from Him, the divine authority is lost to the ministry. But the chain cannot be broken. It has never been a-wanting. The Master Himself, the author of our faith, still lives, and the ministry serves under Him in this His own preferred economy. The sound of His feet is heard behind them. They do what He would be doing were He here, blowing the trumpets of alarm, lifting up their voice for God, publishing the good news from the far-away country, looking for the lost.

And it is a special feature of their official work that they speak to men on His behalf. Preaching is the thing in chief in this Economy, not ritual, not studied scenic effect, not the blare of sound, not architecture, not any complicated machinery, not guilds and brotherhoods, but preaching. It has "pleased God by the foolishness of preaching to save them that believe."

And this is a point of contrast between the ministry of the religion of the Son of God and the priests of the past. Theirs were the smoking altars, and the knives of sacrifice, and the swinging censers, and the endless routine, all of which belong to the religion of the outward. The functions of this later dispensation of the Spirit are other than theirs. Now, we are commissioned to plead with our fellowmen on God's behalf, to use the tongue which is the glory of man in an effort to win them all for Him. "As ye go, preach," is the command. We speak, and we are the only animal that does. Our God speaks, and He is the only Deity that does. Jesus spake on the mountain-top, from the stern of the boat, to the men on the road, in the synagogue, in the Temple. This was His method and His glory, and the ministry is His glory in that He is heard through them. And His line is nearest to parallel with that of the Son of God, who, with the equipment of the Holy Ghost, and with the oil of His formal anointing upon Him, runs to this lost world with the messages of mercy.

There never has been an Economy like this under which we are. There never was a NOW like this, never such a full-tide glory as this noon of this Gospel day. Indeed, it makes the greatest matter under which king we serve, under what conditions we play our part and do our life-work. No Jewish priest, even though mitred, and though attired in the holy garments, filled any such niche as he fills under the Gospel, who is the glory of Christ, and who serves amid these stately sanctities of the New Covenant. The ancient priest stood in the shade and wrought in the twilight, and saw almost nothing that lay beyond that near, wide rim which fenced Judea off from the dark-wide world without. It was, indeed, a long line in which He registered, and it had nothing as its equal or its like in the earth anywhere. And it may well be that but for that ancient priesthood, and that religion with which it was interwoven, the Church of to-day would have been impossible. It was all of God, and had a splendor and a use of its own, so that we owe it much. But it is better to be now, better to serve now as a minister, and to be in so serving the "glory of the Son of God."

III. The Christian ministry is the glory of Christ also in this, that they serve in the last Economy of all.

We have received "a kingdom which cannot be moved," says the apostle. Whatever view be taken of the coming of the Lord, whether it will be before or after the Millennium, it is certain that at the close of the present era of grace Jesus will appear. So that the ministry is His in an important sense, His forerunner, heralding Him, breaking up His way, saying to the people that they should believe on Him who is coming after, that is on Christ Jesus. We, unworthy we, limp, limited, naught in ourselves, are serving Him under the urgency of the last times with a globe upon our hands, for the evangelization of which we are responsible, not reached yet by at least eight hundred and fifty millions of its immortal tenantry. All the lack of the old Mosaic Economy can be easily made good by this which has followed it. It carried in itself the seeds and pledges of its own decay. The moths. God's moths, which had waited so long for the priestly robes of glory and beauty, came at last to fret them away. But lack now in us who are at work in this crowning Economy is final lack, so far as we can see. So that the pressure upon the evangelical ministry of to-day is great indeed. And they are the glory of Christ largely in this very fact.

We are just now upon the edge not of a new year only, but of the new century. The much that has been already done, and of which your pastor made such admirable mention this morning, suggests the more that remains to be done. Everywhere, in these later years, the haste and push are very great along all the lines. And who shall say how far all this may be indicative of the quick coming of the end.

"THE ADVANTAGES OF A LONG PASTORATE."

BY

REV. WM. H. LOGAN.

I am very happy to be with you on this interesting occasion, and congratulate both pastor and people on having lived together for thirty years in ecclesiastical bonds, which are almost as sacred as the marriage tie. Having been acquainted with this Church nearly all my life; my sisters being connected with it, and my wife having been a member of it three different times, and being very intimately acquainted with the pastor for thirty years, it is only natural that I should feel a very deep interest in this celebration, and gladly add what I can to the general rejoicing.

It was also my privilege to preach the last sermon in the old church before it was taken down to give place to this handsome and convenient edifice.

My first recollection of Carlisle was in being taken by my mother to the old Seceder church, on West street, and trying to peer over the high-backed pews at Rev. Mr. Simpson before my feet could touch the floor. Being born and bred in the deepest-blue Presbyterianism, and taught to sing the Psalms in Rouse's version (though it would bother me now to line them out), I have come by inheritance, as well as by mature judgment, to the firm conviction that Presbyterianism is the best form of Church Government and Polity on earth.

By the way, the Seceder Church in this town disappeared long ago—its members either going to Heaven or to the Old School Presbyterian Church; but there is a tradition that many of them thought Mr. McGill was "a little off color" when he left them to become pastor at the corner of Hanover and Pomfret streets.

As the pastorate of Dr. Norcross has been such a long one—covering nearly half the years of the existence of the Second Church—perhaps an appropriate topic for me to discuss in the short time allotted me would be "The Advantages of a Long Pastorate."

While permanency is so desirable, the fact is that in all the Churches adopting the permanent pastorate, the average pastorate does not much exceed the term limit of five years, which obtains in some of the Churches which adopt the itinerancy.

Many things conspire to render the pastorate insecure. Insufficient support is perhaps the chief source of this unrest. Young men who begin with small churches want to do better for themselves. When a man has preached three or five years in a place he often feels that he has about exhausted his mental resources on that people, and that he has presented all the chief heads of theology, and in another field he can use his acquired capital with freshness and added experience. Then the easy facilities of travel; the long vacation; the desire of novelty; the constand trend of population to the large towns and cities, where so many social, literary, musical and æsthetic advantages are to be enjoyed, all tend to render men discontented with what seems the slow and steady grind of three new addresses every week, with little apparent result, and scarcely ever a fellow-minister to come to their relief.

No profession demands such a constant and steady drain on the intellectual resources and sympathies of a man as the ministry, when, at least, three times a week he must appear before the same audience with something new and interesting. The lawyer, the physician, the lecturer, the teacher, has a new audience frequently, or a concrete subject, but the minister generally addresses the same audience and has to preach on an abstract theme.

It is easy to get both subjects and abundance of matter, and it is a joy and delight to preach when there is a lively religious interest in the congregation; but when weeks and months go by, and there is not an inquirer, and the minister hears no word of comment on his preaching, except perhaps criticism, it is not surprising that his courage flags, and he looks with longing eyes to another field. Then, with most men, there is the limitation of abilities to interest and instruct the average congregation for a long time; and the recognition of this fact is doubtless the principal reason for the adoption of the itinerancy. Education greatly aids a man's intellectual resources, but it does not wholly supply his natural limitations.

In addition to all this, there are the defects of the people. After all, Churches are human, and sometimes more human than humane with their ministers. They set a standard both for the man and his abilities far higher than actually exists, and expect him to come up to it. Then, when they are so unresponsive to preaching; often divided among themselves; give him so little spiritual help; are not punctual in his temporal support, and make his patient ear the receptacle of so many complaints, and expect him to approve their side of all contentions, is it any wonder there are so many short pastorates? Paul was burdened with the care of all the churches, and Moses shrank from the labor of leading Israel to the Land of Promise.

Of course, there are splendid compensations in the honor, respect and love that is so generally accorded to ministers, and, above all, the consciousness that he is serving a blessed Master, and engaged in the noblest and most exalted calling, and in the joy of turning many from sin to holiness. But ministers are only human, and do not always live, as they ought, in the high, clear atmosphere of faith.

Many other causes might be mentioned which tend to shorten the pastorate, one specially, the general law that the strong and aggressive men gravitate to the more influential churches, but any way you take it, frequent changes are an injury to a church. The permanent pastorate has decided advantages both to minister and people.

The men who have had the greatest permanent influence have been those who remained longest in one charge. Many men have done good work, and been popular, who only spent a short time in a place; but their influence and work has not been permanent and conserved like those who remained longer. Carlisle Presbytery has had a notable list of long pastorates. Rev. James Snodgrass, of Hanover Church, was perhaps the longest, 1788 to 1846, fifty-eight years—his whole ministerial life. Hanover Church has disappeared from the list of churches, because the whole congregation emigrated. James Sharon, of Paxton and Derry, thirty-six years. Dr. Creigh, of blessed memory, Mercersburg, forty-nine years. Dr. Davidson, First Church, Carlisle, 1785–1812, twenty-seven years. David Denny, Falling Springs, Chambersburg, 1800–1838, thirty-eight years. Dr. DeWitt, Harrisburg, forty-seven years. John Elder, Paxton, fifty-three years. Robert S. Grier, Tom's Creek and Piney Creek, fifty-one years. James Harper, Shippensburg, thirty years. Rev. Dr. John King, Mercersburg, 1769–1811, forty-two years. Robert Kennedy, Welsh Run and Presbytery, forty years. John Linn, Upper and Centre, forty-two years. Dr. McConaughey, Gettysburg, 1800–1832, thirty-two years. Amos McGinley, Path Valley, 1803–1851, forty-eight years. John Moodey, Middle Spring, 1803–1854, fifty-one years. Robert

McCachren, Newville, 1831–1851, twenty years. George Morris, Silver Spring, 1840–1860, twenty years. Jos. A. Murray, Monaghan, 1841–1858, seventeen years. A. D. Mitchell, Paxton, 1850–1874, twenty-four years. Wm. Paxton, Marsh Creek, forty-nine years. T. H. Robinson, Harrisburg, thirty years. John Steel, of Carlisle, " the fighting parson" of the last century, 1759–1779, twenty years. Joshua Williams, Big Spring, 1802–1829, twenty-seven years. James C. Watson, Gettysburg, 1832–1849, seventeen years. N. Grier White, McConnellsburg, thirty years. C. P. Wing, First Church, Carlisle—pastor, twenty-seven years; pastor emeritus, twelve years—thirty-nine years. Robert Cathcart, York, fifty-six years. John Craighead, Rocky Spring, 1768–1799, thirty-one years.

Among the ministers still living there have been many long pastorates: Dr. S. C. Alexander, fourteen years in Upper Path Valley and twelve years in Millerstown. Rev. Dr. J. A. Crawford, Falling Spring, twenty years pastor and thirteen pastor emeritus—thirty-three years, Dr. Geo. S. Chambers, Pine Street, twenty years. Dr. E. Erskine, Newville, twenty-nine years. Rev. J. Smith Gordon, Lower Path Valley, forty-one years. Rev. Dr. Jas. F. Kennedy, in the Presbytery, fifty years. Rev. Wm. McCarrell, Shippensburg, twenty-three years. Dr. George Norcross, thirty years. Dr. S. W. Reigart, Mechanicsburg, twenty-one years. Rev. W. S. Van Cleve, Marsh Creek, thirty years. Rev. W. A. West, Upper Path Valley, twenty—Westminster, seventeen—in Presbytery—forty-five years. Rev. S. S. Wylie, Middle Spring, twenty-seven years.

This is a list of forty names, and perhaps others could be added of men who have served single churches from seventeen to fifty-eight years within the one-time bounds of Carlisle Presbytery. With a few exceptions, the churches they served, or are serving, are the strong, substantial churches of to-day.

Just here I would call attention to an article in *The Presbyterian*, of December 7, 1898, entitled "A Worthy Record," in which the writer refers to the long pastorates in the Southern Church of men still living, and mentions among others Dr. Armstrong, of Norfolk, Va., who has been pastor for forty-seven years; Dr. Moses D. Hoge, of Richmond, Va., fifty-three years; Dr. Palmer, of New Orleans, forty-two years; Dr. Burgett, of Mobile, thirty-nine years; Dr. Jas. R. Graham, of Winchester, Va., forty-seven years; Dr. Jos. B. Stratton, of Natchez, Miss., fifty five years; Dr. Ch. H. Read, of Richmond, Va., forty-nine years, and many others.

Ministers of national and lasting reputation have remained a long time in one church. Dr. Talmage was twenty-five years in the Brooklyn Tabernacle; Henry Ward Beecher preached for forty years in Brooklyn; Dr. Richard S. Storrs has been fifty-three years in the Church of the Pilgrims, Brooklyn; Dr. John Hall was thirty years in the Fifth Avenue Church, New York; Dr. Cuyler was about thirty years pastor, and is still a vigorous preacher and writer; Albert Barnes was nearly forty years pastor of the First Church of Philadelphia. This list could be greatly increased, but enough has been mentioned to show the influence of the long pastorate, both upon the minister and the church.

While some men of very moderate ability and intellectual attainment have remained a long time in a single church, yet they have generally been distinguished for some other traits of character which go to make up the successful pastor, such as personal worth, and acknowledged piety, and great kindness of heart and gentleness. But there is no doubt that the great majority of those who held or are holding these long pastorates are far above the average in abilities—men who stand in the very first rank for intellectual power and consecration to their calling, and who are the peers of any men of the land.

Many of them were exceedingly able men—of large mind and heart, profound scholars, and sometimes of surpassing eloquence—not only distinguished as theologians and ecclesiastics, but men of great literary attainments and true statesmanship, and their influence has long survived them, and is being perpetuated in the men and women trained under their preaching. Their greatest power, however, lay in their fidelity to the Word of God, and in their desire and ability to instruct men in the way of life, rather than in sensation or desire for fame. The closer they kept to the great Commission to preach the Gospel the more lasting the results.

Now, what is there in a long pastorate that helps to make men great and successful preachers?

1. First, we may mention competent support. These men were not serving mission churches, or, at least, they soon came to self-support. They either had their own homes and private means, or their congregations gave them such a support as kept them free from worldly care and avocations. Min-

isters nowhere in this country receive princely salaries, but the poorest policy the Church ever adopts is to require an educated ministry to live on a beggarly salary. Poor support accounts for most of our weak or vacant churches. But when men have been enabled to live in modest comfort— for that is all they have expected or asked—they have worked along contentedly. The very sense of security in their position has stimulated them to give their people the best product of their brains and hearts—to feed them on the finest of the wheat from God's storehouse.

This sense of security also gave them the feeling that their life-work was to be done in one church and community. It identified them with the church until they very naturally spoke of the church and people as my church and my people—a sense of real possession. And in the same way the church became identified in the minds of the people with the pastor, until it was known not so much as the First Church of Carlisle, or the Second Church, but was called Dr. Wing's Church or Dr. Norcross' Church. There is great gain in such an identification. The minister's pride in his people is awakened, and he is anxious that they should be worthy of him, and he of them. Such a pastoral relation is not shaken loose by every wind of difficulty that blows, but patience, and tact and charity are exercised, which in the end confirms the relation more securely.

Such a minister comes to know the true circumstances of his people by long acquaintance and more frequent opportunities to gain their confidence. He rejoices in their prosperity, or sympathizes with them in losses and troubles. It takes a long time to gain the confidence of some people, until you know their real circumstances—their temptations or their excellencies. Ministers seldom come to really know their people until they have been with them in some great joy, like at a wedding, or at some great heart-break, as at a funeral. If, on such occasions, he is tactful and sympathetic, the minister finds an open door to their inmost hearts. He can then influence them as he never could before. But years often go by before such opportunities are afforded him. In a ten years' pastorate, however, there will scarcely be a family in the congregation, or in small communities, where the minister will not be at least once, and often frequently the most highly prized friend, because he has brought to them the consolations of the Gospel in their extremest need.

Ministers are specially interested in those who have come into the Church through their ministry—especially if they have frequently consulted them about their spiritual state of mind. It has been a matter of great interest to watch the growth in grace; or of anxiety if there is danger of falling away. And the convert, too, has a special tender spot in his heart for the man who first awakened serious thoughts in his mind, or led him to Christ. Thus there is a mutual interest which leads the minister to set forth the doctrines of saving grace in their greatest simplicity and beauty, for their fruits and results appear to his very eyes.

2. A long pastorate tends to make a minister a broad student of God's word. Naturally, every one preaches what he supposes are the most important doctrines, and if his stay in a place is brief he has not time to set forth all of them. In his next church he will go over practically the same truths; but if he is staying indefinitely he has time to set forth the whole counsel of God. Thus many precious truths are presented to both pastor and people which otherwise would have been overlooked.

The very necessity of bringing forth some new thing from the storehouse of God's word widens his conception, and increases his delight in obtaining the unsearchable riches of Christ. This is the reason that a man can sustain himself, and be an interesting and instructive preacher to the same congregation for a long term of years.

This tends to make him a student. Men are naturally indolent. Intellectual labor is the hardest kind of labor. The average man is only impelled to work by stern necessity. Ministers are not exceptions to this general characteristic. The reasonable expectation of an intelligent people, and the desire to appear creditably before them, are incentives to diligent preparation, as well as the sense of responsibility to the Great Head of the Church, for fidelity in the discharge of his great office. Therefore, he must read and study, and diligent habits must be cultivated. He must be constantly acquiring if he would bring forth things both new and old. His studies, too, will take a wide range. A new book that helps him to interest his people will be read with delight.

Just here it may be said, that one of the best things the Second Church of Carlisle ever did was to begin the collection of a "Pastor's Library" when Dr. Norcross was installed, and take up a collection for it every year since then. This is now, perhaps, the choicest library in the Presbytery. It gave the pastor the means and incentive to buy the books he needed and desired at the time, and in which he was then specially interested. For if you do not read a book when you greatly desire to see it, or if you read when you are not interested in it, it does you little good. This library, and the stimulus to private purchase, has put much of the best thought of the age within his reach, and this Church has reaped the great benefit of his studies in the model sermons he has given you, and it has made him one of the most scholarly, accomplished, forceful and interesting ministers in the Presbyterian Church.

It would be a great blessing and gain if all our churches would establish and maintain pastor's libraries. It would do much to lengthen the pastorate, by giving the minister the means of bringing much fresh, interesting and timely matter into his pulpit ministrations. Then, too, it widens his scope of subjects for conversation in pastoral and social visiting. We naturally talk about things that are fresh in our minds, and which arrest attention. He can often put a good book in the hand of a friend, and cultivate a taste for reading, and make him a more interested listener to his sermons. It is far more satisfactory and stimulating to preach to attentive and intelligent people than to the dull and ignorant.

3. Another advantage of the long pastorate is, that the minister watches the growth and development of the children. He feels a special interest in those he has baptized. As they grow up and come to the Infant Class, and into the Sunday-school and to church, he calls them by their first or pet names, and they associate the church and religion with him, for they really have never known any other pastor, and, in many cases, seldom hear any other minister preach. He becomes interested in their studies, and the choice of a profession, and is often consulted by parents as to the school or college to which they should send their children. Many men and many women owe it to their pastor that they received a liberal education, and hold the honorable position in society they now enjoy. When the minister recognizes a bright boy or girl in the family, and speaks of them approvingly, a gentle hint to parents has induced them to send them to school and start them on the road to wide usefulness or fame. Ministers have ever been the chief promoters of higher education, and there can be no successful common school

education without the High School and the College.

People do not appreciate how much of their education and refinement, and of the amenities of life, they owe to the educated, conscientious ministers. Why, to listen regularly every Sabbath through a course of years to a minister of ability and thorough scholarship, is in itself a liberal education.

4. The development of benevolence is another great advantage of the long pastorate. If you will examine the statistics of the General Assembly you will find that the churches which make the largest contributions to the various Boards and Agencies of the Church are the ones which seldom change pastors. This is notably so in Carlisle Presbytery. When a church is vacant, or frequently has a new pastor, the revenues and benevolence fall off. It usually takes a church at least a year to get a new pastor, and that means a great deal of uncertainty and irregularity. Whereas the regular pastor has stated times or methods for gathering these benevolent offerings. He feels interested to develop the spirit of benevolence among his people. Frequently calls their attention to it, and stimulates them to do better from year to year, and thus the aggregate contributions increase, and his church becomes a

perennial fountain of benevolence. Under this long and faithful instruction the charity of many a saint has been developed. Few people remember their Lord's work in their wills who have not been cheerful contributors to it while living.

5. Another advantage of the long pastorate is, that the people reap the benefit of the ripened learning, observation and experience of their pastor. People generally want an old and experienced lawyer, physician and general, but it is remarkable how many prefer the young and callow preacher. Experience is just as valuable in the preacher as it is in any other calling or profession. Trials, failures, successes, teach us a great many useful lessons. The pastor of observation, experience and prudence avoids or overcomes many a difficulty, where the rash man would simply butt his head against a stone wall. "Old men for counsel, young men for action."

What relief it is to a church to feel that it has not periodically to select a new minister! Churches do not thrive well on novelty. Brilliant and sensational men never stay long in one place. Neither do men who are technically called revival preachers. They cannot long sustain the high tension of that kind of preaching, and when the special interest or excitement abates, and the affairs of the church move only in the normal way, they get discouraged, and seek another field.

It is only men of endurance—men of equitable temper, who are capable of plodding; who can sow the seed, and be content to wait God's time for the harvest; who are not easily discouraged; who do not need to call in the Presbytery to settle their difficulties; who have not such a high and mighty opinion of their own judgment that their resignation will be tendered if the congregation does not always do what they want done; but who have tact and discretion to bear and forbear—it is only such men who are either fitted by nature or grace to remain long in one church, and render acceptable service. Dr. Jas. L. Valandingham, of New Castle Presbytery, preached at the Head of Christiana church for forty years, during which time three self-sustaining churches grew out of his charge. When he resigned a few years ago it was very truthfully said of him, that the Lord had endowed him with a double portion of good, common sense, or he never could have stayed so long in one place.

It speaks well for the scholarship, industry, fidelity and good sense of a man when the people will bear with his human weaknesses, and listen to him patiently through a long course of years, and it is just as complimentary to a congregation and to their credit that their minister is willing to spend a life time with them, and bear with their murmurings, and neglects, and follies.

It is not to the credit of a congregation to frequently change pastors—they did not make a wise choice, or have not treated him well. On the score of human weakness "honors are very easy" between pastors and people. It is usually well for both to remember the wisdom of Hamlet and

> rather bear those ills we have,
> Than fly to others that we know not of.

Among the sisterhood of Churches the Presbyterian stands conspicuous for the formation of character, for the development of individual liberty, responsibility and personal worth. A man has no better passport to confidence and respectful consideration than to have it said of him, "He is a consistent member of the Presbyterian Church." Though Presbyterians are not the largest body numercially (standing perhaps 5th or 6th), yet they are doing more than the fourth part of all the Foreign Mission work of the world, and are by far the largest contributors to the general benevolence of the world.

The doctrine of Divine Sovereignty; the educated ministry, and the permanent pastorate have been the chief factors in developing and sustaining such a character. No other church can show such a general high average character of her individual membership. The influences are mutual. The doctrine and polity tends and aims to build up such a character, and people of clear heads, who do their own thinking, are drawn to such a church. Thus it comes to pass that Presbyterians everywhere have their denominational stamp, and they are proud of it, and it is no small privilege and honor to be a member of such a church, or to be permitted to minister to them. Men like Dr. Archibald Alexander and Dr. Samuel Miller, who were each forty years, and Dr. Charles Hodge who was fifty years, instructors in Princeton Seminary, have left an indelible impression on the ministry and membership of the whole Presbyterian denomination.

'6. Did time permit, we could speak of the value of the long pastorate to the Presbytery. As a rule, the men who have given character and reputation to the Presbytery have been those who have been longest in service. Their faces became familiar to the churches. They were honored and respected, and the community accepted their deliverances as wise and prudent. Amid the constant changes going on in Presbytery, how often we hear people say, "We don't know many of the ministers now." The familiar faces and voices of the fathers are gone, and it is said, "We don't know the new men." Thus the social power of the Presbytery declines, and doubtless this is one reason why churches are not more anxious to entertain the Presbytery—it is not like a meeting of old friends.

The Christian ministry is the most exalted and responsible office among men. Paul regarded it as the greatest grace of Christ to him; and his consuming desire was to be found faithful to his trust. His reward was the approval of his Master, and the conversion of many souls. So the man who, through many years, has been the religious guide and instructor of his people; who has "allured men to heaven, and led the way," is worthy of all congratulation and honor. Happy in doing good, and imitating his Master, "he ne'er has changed or wished to change his place." Men gladly rise up and do him honor.

"WHAT I KNOW ABOUT THIS CHURCH AND PASTOR."

BY

REV. W. T. L. KIEFFER.

My personal acquaintance with this church dates back to 1867. I was then a timid youth, with strong innate Presbyterian proclivities, which caused me occasionally to play truant from the Reformed Church, where my family belonged, and drop into a rear pew in the old Second Presbyterian Church to hear Dr. Bliss preach. Personal acquaintance with the pastor, whose thirtieth anniversary we are now observing, began in the winter of 1873; and during the summer of that year I transferred my membership to this church while a student at Princeton Theological Seminary. This church and pastor have thus been most intimately associated with my ministerial life; and it is with the greatest pleasure that I now bear filial testimony to their worth to me. Our acquaintance and friendship cover almost the period made prominent by this anniversary service; and supply some sort of warrant for me to hint at

"What I Know About this Church and Pastor"—the theme which has been assigned me.

I am glad this is not a funeral; and that I am not this evening in the position of the minister I recently read of, who had been engaged by an eccentric man to preach his funeral sermon in his presence while still living. The man wanted to know what would be said about him, and declared it to be his intention to demand strict honesty of the preacher, and if he should either overstate or understate the truth about him, he would then and there rise and contradict him, as he could not if he waited till he was dead! He had heard so much unwarranted panegyric at funerals that he wanted no lying at his. Though I neither desire nor intend to exaggerate or minify, and have not been threatened with instant correction in either case, yet I am glad this is not a funeral, not even by way of anticipation. The happy circumstances of the occasion are such as would disparage overstatement, and atone for understatement of fact.

One is strongly impressed with the mutual influence of church and pastor on each other during so prolonged association. The old adage, "Like priest like people," finds its counterpart in its own reverse,

"Like people like priest." They are mutually affected. In the present instance we find marks of strong individuality on both sides. This church was born with a positive temperament; and has retained it. So, too, the pastor. And whilst the pastor has contributed much towards making this church what it is, the church has done its share in developing the pastor. This double-acting relationship must not be forgotten as we look for points. I know not what this church might have become under another pastor or pastors, nor what thirty years in another church, or in other churches, might have made this pastor; but I know this, that together these two have grown to splendid character, service and honor in the Master's kingdom. It is much to the credit of both that they have mutually appreciated each other's merits, borne with their faults, loved and been loved, helped and been helped during these long years. This harmony of two positive temperaments is an object-lesson to all churches and pastors in these days of unrest, when the lack of forbearance causes so many needless pastoral changes.

Among the things I know about this church and pastor are these, and such as these:

1. They have been RELIGIOUSLY AGGRESSIVE.

They have stood for something. This pulpit has given no uncertain sound on the issues that differentiate the Church from the world. The pew occupants have had no occasion to rate the Church of Christ a mere social club; but have been faithfully taught to align themselves with the Gospel. This is a church, not a philosophical, nor theosophical, nor scientific society; but a church, whose mission is the religious culture of souls. It is a church, not a social entertainment agency, without spiritual intent.

Consequently, it has been aggressive and progressive in its religious life. Worldliness has left its soiled finger-marks on it, to be sure, as on others; but, in spite of it, the tone and effort of the church have been in the direction of positive religion. This is an important fact and factor. For many churches and ministers are spiritually inefficient, because they stand for nothing, and do nothing distinctively religious. Such has become the terrorism of worldliness in the church over the pulpit that many pastors fear to insist on religion; and so the church loses its power, and degenerates into an ambiguity.

I know that whatever may be the measure of secularity hereabouts, it has not been permitted to consume the vital energy of this church, because the leader has set too agressive a step for its religious life. With excellent tact and fidelity the fundamental principles of practical religion have been declared, and real godliness has been inculcated. The result shows the value of such steadfastness and agressiveness. It is a sign of disease and decline when ministers lose their spiritual caste and yield themselves to irreligion. The church has a great work to do; and should be about it.

2. I know this church and pastor have been ORTHODOX.

No theological fungus has had a chance to grow around the edges of this pulpit. The "New Theology" has not been able to get in edgewise or otherwise. Higher Criticism has not been able to cast a cloud over the minds of the people. The old light has burned too brightly for that. The "fads" have come and gone; but the old story has been told in the old way. The heresy-hunter has had no call hither. This pulpit has been rockribbed in its orthodoxy.

I cannot think of a better thing to say than this on this occasion. Loyalty to revealed truth is a noble quality. It is needed now as much as it was in the martyr-days, around which gathers such a halo of glory. There has been such a persistent pecking at the foundations of our belief, during recent years, that the timid have been alarmed and the unsteady have faltered. Men have almost, if not altogether, mocked at those who have dared to adhere to the old doctrines. They have claimed all the scholarship worth naming; and have relegated to antiquity's dusty shelf the doctrines and beliefs that made our forefathers strong and brave and successful in the Master's work.

But none of such nonsense has obtained here. This Church has appreciated the high scholarship of its pastor; and has no need to hanker after the theological autocrats who would make them dissatisfied. Here the Gospel has been proclaimed to sinner and saint with that clearness of interpretation and that fulness of faith and boldness of utterance which could not foster anything else than loyal allegiance thereto. This pastor is a scholar, and knows how to think; and this church knows it. Who could doubt his Presbyterianism? Know we not all how true he has been to our Standards? "Doctrinal Sermons" have not brought hysteria nor dyspepsia to the people awake, nor nightmare to the people asleep, as seems to be the case in some other churches. Nor have the sermons always been short, dandy-like affairs. They have been preached whenever required and in such way as indicated that the preacher himself had a good grip on the truth and must tell it. His own knowledge and faith and loyalty have therefore been imparted to the people; and that is why this church has had and has such good "stuff" in it. The people have been fed on the Gospel and have grown on the diet. The strong meat has made them strong.

Who doubts this pastor's Protestantism? Does any follower of Leo XIII hereabouts question his evangelical fibre? There is no ground for the least suspicion as to his alignment with the Reformation; and this church, magnanimous withal towards all beliefs and methods, cannot be indifferent to the issues that demarcate Protestantism from its historic opponent. Presbyterians here at least have no reason to be ignorant as to why they are Protestant.

The same loyalty to Gospel principles is seen in all moral questions that the day brings forward. Temperance and social order have had no braver, more earnest, or more prudent advocate than that occupying this pulpit. And it could not be otherwise than that the predominant sentiment of this church should be set in the same direction. This pulpit, strong, clear, and brave in its own beliefs, has helped shape the opinion and practice of its adherents. Not that every one always thought as the pulpit taught; for that would be impossible. But the caste of opinion and belief has been given by the pulpit in the direction of orthodoxy in both belief and practice. And there is great honor in that.

3. I know this church and pastor have been BENEVOLENT.

Anyone who glances over the Assembly Minutes for all these years will quickly see that this church has been liberal in its benevolences, and has steadily advanced therein, according to its current financial ability. Though church and manse have been built and practically rebuilt at great outlay, yet all the Boards have been generously and continuously supported; and this church's record need bring it no blush of shame as it confronts it. When we ministers wish to know something about a strange church, we first look at its record in the Assembly Minutes;

and not infrequently we find churches with large enrollment making a very shabby report on the benevolence question ; and we conclude that something is wrong with said church or it would show larger benevolent contributions. Usually this is the key to the character and efficiency of the church. Any one making this search would at once decide that the Second Church of Carlisle is a good church, whose machinery is well oiled and in excellent working order. If ever it becomes vacant—and may that day be remote—an inrush of applicants may be expected, which will sweep the Elders off their feet, if they do not properly brace themselves against it ; for all the restless preachers in the kingdom will jump at so good a place. That is one of the consequences of being a wide-awake church in these important matters.

But here again we see that this church could not well help being liberal. For has not this pastor for thirty years been teaching, exhorting and leading the people in all the lines of Gospel beneficence ? Missionary to the core—Scriptural in method—fearless and persistent in service, he has made it difficult and uncomfortable for people to lag behind. Years ago one of his parishioners was wont, in a jocular way, sometimes to remark on Sabbath morning, about church-time, "Well, I guess we must go down and listen to another sermon on Giving, or Missions." The oft-preached themes may not have been any too attractive to him; but faithful, strong, tactful preaching inevitably filtered through to the quick of the heart, and so reached the purse.

It is not given to every minister of the Gospel thus to provoke and direct the benevolence of people. There is some special endowment required for it. This pastor has the gift, and he has used it with excellent effect. The quickening has been wholesome; and this church, rejoicing to-day in its strength, owes much to this very stimulation it has received from the pastor in all works of benevolence. The story is told of a boy who accidentally swallowed a silver coin. Alarm instantly seized the family. The cry sounded, "Run for the doctor; quick, run for the doctor." But a lad who was present said, "No; run for our preacher, for I heard pop say *he could get money out of anybody.*" So characteristic of our pastor is this eminent ability as a money-extractor that the suspicion grows on me this story must have originated in the Second church. Anyhow, God be praised that His people here have followed their leader, and have not withheld their substantial offerings, but have freely given them in tribute to His grace. Thus have they been blessed, and been made strong and happy in His service.

4. I know this church and pastor have been content with the Gospel ordinances as the means of growth and advancement.

This pulpit has not had to resort to any of the various devices of sensationalism, which have become common in some places. "Picture-Sermons," whose familiar advertising circulars we oft receive, have not been required here to gain patronage. Fancy-concerts, with a sermonette attachment, have not figured as the church's hope of good standing and usefulness in the community. Reliance has been placed upon the faithful preaching of the Word, the straightforward and earnest telling of "the old, old story." This is in direct conformity to Gospel counsel and precedent, and here the blessing of God has attended this means and method of work.

There is no substitute for preaching. Due recognition and place must of course be given other parts of public worship and other associated agencies. But after all this remains the hope of the church's progress. Attempts at substitution have come to grief. Churches fed on the husks of sensationalism have narrowed and failed. It is said that in a certain city many of the churches are resorting to various ingenious devices in the way of sacred concerts, and similar appliances, to attract people to the evening service, small allowance of time and interest being given the sermon. But it is also said that the greatest number of additions to the membership is found in those churches, in that same city, whose main reliance has been on the plain Gospel ordinances, and which have honored preaching as God's appointed means and method of grace. They may not have had the crowd nor the hurrah; but the savor of the Gospel was with them, and souls were reached by the truth, the only thing that can quicken them. Salvation, not entertainment, is the watchword of the honest pastor and church; and the Word only can make "wise unto salvation." There is room for the exercise of the best gifts in making preaching attractive, as it ought to be made, that it may address the intellect, appeal to the heart, and move the will. The best preacher must oft say, "Who is sufficient for these things?" But it is noteworthy that the preachers who have risen to lasting honor have been devoutly evangelical, and have trusted in the divine Word to work that spiritual sensation which lost souls require.

Our congratulations and rejoicings today are accentuated by the fact that here again the old Gospel has been honored and that its saving efficacy has been demonstrated. How cheap and foolish all species of ecclesiastical claptrap must seem beside this! We honor our brother as a preacher, reverent, intellectual, warm-hearted, unwearying; and we rejoice this day to do him honor. Blessed indeed are they whose privilege it has been and is to sit under his ministrations; and be led into the knowledge of God's truth. May the day never come to this beloved Zion when faithful Gospel preaching shall be depreciated or become the occasion of discontent and unrest.

Such are some of the things I know and you know about this church and pastor,—things which deserve to be said on this occasion. I know how conservative both are; but that very conservatism is excellent ballast and assures the progress of the work. They are both up to the times in all that affects the kingdom and cannot stand still or go back.

I know the influence of this pastor has gone out

from this church far hence. We who have enjoyed his love and confidence and counsel, and have gone into the ministry—even to foreign lands—have carried with us the impress of his training and have thus extended his influence. The fact is worth noting that eight young men have entered the ministry from this church during this pastorate. Of these two have been Foreign Missionaries, and two Home Missionaries. This church has also in this time supplied seven minister's wives, three of whom are Presbyterian, three Methodist Episcopal, and one Protestant Episcopal. The Bible says "A good wife is from the Lord." But I doubt not the other favored ministers will join me in adding the words —"and from the Second Church!" Nor will there be dissent from the opinion that our matrimonial fortune has been simply patterned after that of this church's pastor, or that to his excellent helpmeet we are indebted for much of the wise helpfulness brought us by our own. We are only giving honor to whom honor is due, when we credit much of the success of this church and pastor to the cultured and prudent wife who has shared the lights and shadows of the pastorate with him. Both directly and indirectly she has been a factor in the glad success we celebrate today. Surely none of us would, if we could, ever forget the helpful fellowship of this church and pastor in days agone. Speaking for those who are not here, I would pay this affectionate tribute to him and you. Wherever we go and among whomsoever we live and labor, we shall ever appreciate the Providence that linked our lives with yours in religious fellowship and service: and our prayer is that we may never be a dishonor to you.

It was said this afternoon, "The Past is secure; what of the Future?" For this we have no anxiety. The principles and practices which have made the Past will abide and mould the Future. Social conditions may change and bring new difficulties into the work; but this church and pastor have the requisite power of adaptation to conditions which will issue in success. The Scotch-Irish element may wane, and others, not historically Presbyterian, may take its place; but I believe this power of adjustment and assimilation will continue to mould diverse materials into the one distinctive congregational life. In that lies the outlook of our churches through this region; and that will assure this church's perpetual vigor.

The sociologist is often perplexed over the disposal of the complex multitudes that come to America for settlement; and is often worried lest overdone immigration work ultimate ruin to our national institutions. But he is a dull student who does not observe the unique power of assimilation possessed by America. We look abroad and see that in England a native is always an Englishman; in Scotland a Scotchman; in Ireland an Irishman; in Germany a German; and so on. Who thinks of anything else than this? But behold them all, and other nameless hordes, coming here, and thrown into the national hopper, with the result of a grist in a generation or two that is distinctively American! True, it is a trifle hard on the hopper at times; but the grist is always a successful blending of the antecedent types. In that lies the hope of our country. And in that power of assimilation of other than hereditary Presbyterians lies the future success of this church. Pride of ancestry and achievement can only be mischievous, if relied on for future advancement. Faithful and indefatigable work alone can and will assure the future.

Thirty years! How rich their memory! How

strong and far-reaching their influence for good! What augury of great things to come! We, who have long been away, are practically strangers among you to-day; but we remember the past, we trust the future. This is the first thirty-year pastorate Carlisle has had; and Carlisle Presbytery has now only one pastor in service with a longer term to his credit, viz.: Rev. J. Smith Gordon, of Lower Path Valley, who has been forty years in that charge. As the years roll on, may they be as fruitful of good as these thirty have been; and when the end comes, may the victory of faith be ours, and we rejoice with unspeakable joy in the great coronation, toward which we all look and work, in that eternity where the years are not counted, and anniversaries are only a pleasant memory!

ADDRESSES.

Monday Afternoon, January 2, 1899.

REV. EBENEZER ERSKINE, D. D.,
NEWVILLE, PA.,
PRESIDING.

Dr. Erskine expressed his personal appreciation of the spirit in a congregation which observed such an anniversary as this. He hoped it might catch in other churches, and come nearer home. He had known the pastor of this church before his settlement in Carlisle. They had been members of the same Synod in the West. The first time they met as members of the same judicatory was in the fall of 1865, when the Synod of Chicago was convened in the city of Galena. Dr. Erskine was then just establishing the "*North-Western Presbyterian*" in the great Metropolis of the West, a Church paper, which was afterwards changed to the "*Interior*." The pastor of this church was at that time a young man, who had been recently ordained and installed in his first charge at North Henderson, Mercer county, Ill.

The attention of Dr. Erskine was first called to the young man by an earnest speech which he made in this meeting of Synod on one of the burning questions of the day. As the young man agreed with Dr. Erskine, the latter naturally concluded that he was a man of promise, and one that ought to be encouraged. Subsequently he desired to have him settled in Chicago as pastor over what has since become the Fifth Presbyterian Church of that city, and he was instrumental in procuring a call for him to that new enterprise, a fact which is here gratefully recorded. But the young man preferred the call to Carlisle, and here he began his work thirty years ago.

It is idle to guess what would have been the result of his going to Chicago at that time; he might have had a more active and conspicuous life; he might have been in his grave long ago. We do not know what "might have been," we only know what the kind Providence of God has brought to both. By His great loving kindness, Dr. Erskine and his "young friend" have been called to work side by side in this delightful valley for almost all these thirty years. Their ministerial exchanges have been very pleasant and profitable, and when in 1886 the Presbytery of Carlisle celebrated its Centennial they were associated in the labor of preparing for and carrying out that important anniversary. The occasion resulted in the publication of "THE CENTENNIAL MEMORIAL" which is a complete History of Carlisle Presbytery,—a work of permanent value not only in this locality but to the Church at large. In this labor of love were associated the three friends, West, Erskine and Norcross, who wrought patiently together until their work was accomplished and given to the world in 1890.

The speaker said he was very happy in being present at this anniversary, and he extended his hearty congratulations to both pastor and people on the work that had been accomplished in this congregation. He then introduced the speakers in the order of the programme.

"THE IDEAL CHURCH."

BY

REV. WM. A. McCARRELL.

Before coming here I did not know exactly what the nature of this service was to be—especially did I not know what the character of the addresses was to be—whether grave or gay, pathetic or profound.

I certainly shall not make the last mentioned kind. The only limitation put upon me, however, was by our good brother, Dr. Norcross, who told me that I was to say very little about him. Why this was, I do not know. It may be that he was afraid to trust me. Certainly he will not object to my congratulating him on the grand record he has made here, and, he will not object to my congratulating this church on the grand record it has made during these thirty years of happy pastoral relation.

So far as Dr. Norcross is concerned, I am free to confess I feel towards him very much like that Spanish Senorita, with whom the celebrated Tom Corwin is said to have come in contact several years ago in Havana. According to the story, he was taking dinner in the then Spanish capital of Cuba. He happened to be sitting beside a Spanish lady of the first rank. When the coffee was brought to the table, the Senorita proceeded to pour molasses into it. Mr. Corwin begged her to stop pouring as she would have it too sweet for him. "Ah," said she with her blandest smile, "If it were *all* molasses it would not be too sweet for *you*." So I feel that if this service were to be all congratulation it would not be too sweet for this pastor and this people. They both deserve to be congratulated. But I forbear, remembering the injunction laid upon me. I am to say a few words this afternoon concerning the "Ideal Church."

This is an important subject, and very much might be said on it. It is, however, an ideal which seems to elude one as he tries to grasp it. The first remark I would make, however is, that there *is* an "Ideal Church." *The* Ideal Church is the church —and I am now speaking of individual churches— is the church composed not only of truly converted men and women, together with their children, but of men and of women who are so nearly sanctified that there is but one remove between them and angels. I know that such a church has never as yet been fully realized on earth; it is only seen in "the Church of the First-Born in Heaven;" but I have sometimes thought that in these days of restlessness and desire for change, there are some ministers who are on the look out for such a church. There is always something wrong with the churches where, it is to be taken for granted, the Lord put them. And, on the other hand, there seem to be churches who are on the constant look-out for the "Ideal Minister," i. e., the perfect minister. I have often wondered what such a church and such a minister would do if they were to be brought together. There would be nothing for the minister to do, for the people would already be perfect, and, there would be nothing for the people to do, for there would be nothing about the minister that any one could criticise.

But, while the absolutely ideal church is not attainable in this world, at least before the Millenium, there is an ideal church which is attainable—at least it so seems to me. What is it, then? Let me define it as nearly as I can. The ideal church is a body of professing Christians, banded together, according to God's appointment, for two things: 1. The worship of God, and 2. The service of God.

This may not seem to be, at first thought, a very good definition of the ideal church as attainable in this world; but the more you will think of it the more comprehensive, I think, you will find it to be.

Take the first part of the definition: The ideal church is a body of professing Christians, banded together for the worship of God. There is a vast deal comprehended in that.

1. First of all, in such a church, the honor, the glory of God would be uppermost in the minds of the great majority of the membership. Such a church would not be a mutual admiration society. It would not be a social club— although the highest kind of sociability would exist. The church building would not be a place of fashionable resort, where the milliners and the tailors would get a weekly advertisement. "The rich and the poor would meet together," recognizing the fact that "the Lord was the Maker of them all." When the people came to God's house, it would not be to have their intellectual or aesthetic natures ministered to by deep-rolling organ, operatic singing, or eloquent or *dilettante* preaching, in the ordinary acceptance of those words. The people would come to God's house for the purpose of rendering thanksgiving to

Him for all His goodness to them personally and collectively; for the purpose of confessing sin, and imploring mercy through the grace which is in Christ Jesus—they would come to hear what God, the Lord, had to say to them out of His Word and by the mouth of His ministering servant. And here, in this ideal church, the place of the ideal minister would be evident. He would come into the pulpit, not to receive the applause of men for his literary and eloquent dissertations; not to be flattered by the world for his grace and eloquence, or for the flow of his pulpit robes; but he would come as the messenger of God, as the "ambassador of Christ," to declare the "whole counsel of God, whether men would hear or whether they would forbear."

2. Then, in the second place, in such a church, the great end aimed at by the membership would be a higher spirituality. Like the apostle of old, they "would count themselves not to have already attained, neither to be already perfect, but forgetting the things which are behind, and reaching forth to those things which are before, they would press toward the mark for the prize of the high calling of God in Christ Jesus." Instead of judging one another, the members would, first of all, judge them-

selves. Instead of busying themselves with pulling the motes out of their brother's eye, they would first pull the beams out of their own eyes. Their constant prayer would be, "Create in me a clean heart, O God, and renew a right spirit within me."

All of these things, and more, would necessarily flow out of a church thus banded together for the worship of God, i. e., where the worship of God was one of the great ends sought after. Then, take the second part of the definition of the ideal church— "A body of professing Christians, banded together for the service of God." How much is embraced in that!

1. In the first place, the membership of such a church would ever be possessed of the idea "that they were not their own, but that they had been bought with a price;" not their will, but God's will was to be done. There would then be the hearty consecration of the person and of the substance to the Lord. Doing something for God would be a joy and a privilege, and not a task and a burden. Each one would feel that he was "Christ's bond-servant."

2. Then, in the second place, in such a church, each one would feel that he was bound not to look on his own things merely, but also have

a regard to his "brother's welfare." Each one would strive to help his fellow in the Christian life. There would be the bearing of one another's burdens, and so there would be the fulfilling of the law of Christ. One of the great ends of the Church visible would thus be attained—the helping of one another in the divine life.

3. Then, in the third place, in such a church, devoted to the service of the Lord, those outside of the kingdom would be looked after. There would be earnest prayer for the unsaved. There would be the constant endeavor to get those who do not come to God's house to do so. The membership would be constantly saying to those outside, "Come thou with us, and we will do thee good: for the Lord hath spoken good concerning Israel." For their own spiritual good, for the encouragement of their pastor, for the purpose of drawing others, the membership of such a church would always be in their places in the sanctuary on the Lord's day and in the weekly meeting for prayer, unless providentially hindered. There would be none of the modern "oncers" in such a church.

Then, in such a church, banded together for worship and service, there would be much prayer, both public and private. There would be much prayer for the pastor, that all of his ministrations might be blessed of God; that he might be strengthened and upheld by the power of God. A minister once said to his Deacons, who had complained to him that his work did not seem to prosper as it once did, "The reason is, that I have lost my prayer-book." When his officers wondered at this, he explained: "Once, said he, my people prayed earnestly for me, that I might be prospered in my work; that saints might be edified, and that sinners might be converted; but now, very little or no prayer is made for me, and I can do nothing." Is this not the secret of many a church's deadness?

Then, such a church, devoted to the service of God, will remember that its commission is world-wide. It will remember the great command of its Master, "Go ye into all the world and preach the Gospel to every creature." I cannot conceive of an ideal church which is not a missionary church. The narrow cry of "Heathen enough at home!" will never be heard in such a church. On the other hand, its cry will be, "The world for Christ and Christ for the world!"

In such a church, pastor and people will be bound

together by the ties of mutual love and forbearance. The people will look up to their undershepherd as their God-appointed teacher and leader, remembering that he is responsible, not to *them*, but to the Great Head of the Church. Pastor and people will alike seek the glory of God the Father and the honor of Jesus Christ His Son, and striving to serve God here below, they will look forward to that glad day when the worship and service of the Church on earth will give place to the higher worship and service of the Church in Heaven! Is this ideal attainable here and now? I fully believe it is. All our churches need is a fresh and mighty baptism of the Holy Spirit, and all I have spoken of may be and will be attained.

May that baptism come speedily! And may you, my dear brother, and you, his devoted people, realize as never before the "Ideal Church." That picture presented by Longfellow in his "Children of the Lord's Supper," comes as near, as it seems to me, "The Ideal Church" as anything on earth can be. We can only quote a few words. Having described the church and the surroundings, he goes on to describe the service. He says:

"Loud rang the bells already; the thronging crowd was
    assembled
Far from valleys and hills to list to the holy preaching,
Hark! then roll forth at once the mighty tones from the
    organ,
Hover like the voices from God, aloft, like invisible spirits,
Like as Elias in heaven, when he cast off from him his
    mantle,
Even so cast off the soul its garments of earth; and with
    one voice
Chimed in the congregation, and sang an anthem immortal
Of the sublime Wallin, of David's harp in the North-Land
Tuned to the choral of Luther; the song on its powerful
    pinions
Took every living soul, and lifted it gently to heaven.
And every face did shine like the Holy One's face upon
    Tabor.
Lo! there entered then into the church the Reverend
    Teacher.
Father by right, and he was in the Parish; a christianly
    plainness
Clothed from his head to his feet the old man of seventy
    winters.
Friendly was he to behold, and glad as the heralding angel
Walked he among the crowds, but still a contemplative
    grandeur
Lay on his forehead as clear, as on moss-covered grave-
    stone a sun beam.
As in his inspiration (an evening twilight that faintly
Gleams in the human soul, even now, from the day of crea-
    tion)
Th' artist, the friend of heaven, imagines saint John when
    in Patmos,
Gray, with his eyes uplifted to heaven, so seemed then the
    old man;

Such was the glance of his eye, and such were his tresses of
  silver.
All the congreation arose in the pews that were numbered.
But with a cordial look, to the right and to the left hand,
  the old man
Nodding all hail and peace disappeared in the innermost
  chancel."

What a picture of the Ideal Church this is! Pastor and people bound together in the bonds of Christ's love! The people reverencing and looking up to the Pastor as the minister and messenger of God; looking up to him as their counsellor and friend; reverencing him more and more as the days go by, and, when his locks begin to whiten, seeing in them that crown of glory which comes to a godly old age, and which is a type of that "Crown of Righteousness" which fadeth not away.

And so may you, my dear brother, and you his faithful people be bound together until the Great Head of the Church Himself shall loose the bond and bid this pastor, "Come up higher!"

"THE PASTOR'S BAND."

BY

REV. H. G. STOETZER.

Scripture, history and recent events teach the great truth, that God is marching on, and in the beautiful lines of one,

> "He has sounded forth the trumpet that shall never call retreat ;
> He is sifting out the hearts of men before the judgment seat :
> Oh, be swift, my soul, to answer Him ! be jubilant my feet !
> Our God is marching on."

"And there went with him a band of men, whose hearts God had touched." This band refers to a band of men who went with Saul, just anointed King of Israel. They followed loyally the King when others deserted. They served and upheld the King, when the sons of Belial sulked and said, "How shall this man save us ?"

It does no violence to the truth, nor to this occasion, to apply these words to a "Pastor's Band."

This occasion is made possible as much by the loving loyalty, the kindly forbearance and the godly life of the band of men and women, whose hearts God has touched, as by the matchless manhood, the unquestioned scholarship and the undoubted devotion of the pastor, whom we this day delight to honor, for his stainless life, for his unselfish labors, for his wise and tender leadership, and for his faithful exposition and fearless, yet loving, deliverance of God's message to men. Hobson would never have been immortalized without Hobson's heroic crew. There would be no hero of "Rough Riders" without the rugged manhood that bravely followed. Were it not for noble bands of men and women, whose hearts God has touched, long pastorates would be impossible. Were it not for such a loyal band in this church, the pastor, if among the living at all, would likely be laboring in another field.

It is a sad thought to any pastor that this noble, godly band remains uncrowned, unhonored and unsung, but not unknown, either in this world, or by the recording angel, who faithfully notes the lovely lives and unselfish deeds of all those whose hearts God has touched.

Would it were possible to sing the song of their sacrifices, and tell the story of their devotion, but one must be content with the insufficient record of some general characteristics of this and similar bands.

Notice, then 1, their Godly Character; 2, their Unity of Purpose; 3, their Progressive Spirit.

I. They are Godly in Character, because God has touched their hearts, and having touched their hearts,

1. They have life, since God in Christ is Life. When King Midas touched a twig of oak, a stone, or an apple, they turned to gold. We have a King as far above King Midas as the soul is higher and of greater worth than oak or stone or apple. He touched the lifeless form of a poor widow's son and life returned. He touched sin-sick and suffering humanity and made it whole. He laid His loving hand on the frail frame of a feverish woman and the fever left her. One touch of His magic hand clothed the demoniac in his right mind. The poor, despised leper, separated from home and the haunts of men, He touched and restored to home and happiness. At His tender touch the water "blushed," and bread multiplied. The ears of those to whom music had been a stranger opened to His gentle touch, the dumb expressed their gratitude in melodious tones, and the lame leaped for joy. Under the soothing power

and presence of the Great Physician and Healer of all hurts, diseases of body and soul flee, and infirmities depart to return no more.

His work, however, is not simply negative, to dispel weakness, want and woe; He came for the very and only purpose of giving life, which is more than mere living, life at once abundant, joyous and victorious; a life filled with the highest ideals of character and the loftiest aspirations for unselfish service. This life He not merely gives, but sustains by His personal presence, so that each can say with Paul, "I am crucified with Christ; nevertheless I live; yet not I, but Christ, liveth in me." And the life which He began He also completes; for we are complete in Him, and only in Him, and Christ in us is the hope of glory, and the only hope of a present spotless character and final crowning.

2. The Lord of Life gives also Light.

One characteristic of light is to dispel darkness. Since God said: "Let there be light," light has unceasingly chased and vanquished the darkness. And the Light which came, on the blackest night of the world's history, in the form of the seemingly helpless babe of Bethlehem, has been growing greater and brighter in power and splendor; so that to-day there are few lands indeed where there are not some women and men whose hearts have been touched by the spirit of Christ and His Gospel of glad-tidings. He touched with light those highest, at Jerusalem, and they carried the Light of the world to the candles of the Lord in the uttermost parts of the earth. He has been the Light of the lowly and the lofty, so that from His day until now, there has been a light to cheer the weary and point out the way to the lost, and that light will be a beacon until man shall cease and time shall be no more.

As light dispels darkness, coldness, and impurity from the hearts of men, it at the same time reveals duty and purity; and unveils the way men should walk; and discloses new and higher conceptions of life—that gain and enlargement come by losing; increase in knowledge and abiding wisdom by teaching; and growth in greatness through humble service. But Christ demands of those whose hearts have been touched more than service. He demands self, surrendered and consecrated; and the zeal of such souls is mighty and matchless, when they think of the time misspent, the privileges abused, the opportunities neglected, when they remember the judgment with the horror or glory of unending ages, the myriads of dead and dying, with few to wake the dead and rescue the perishing.

Light besides dispelling darkness and unveiling duty beautifies. Without light all would be dull and dark monotony. If God had not enrobed Nature with a garment of light, there would be no blue above us and no green beneath, no "crimson streak on ocean's cheek," no forest as beautiful as an army victorious with the banners of fallen foes, no songsters with many-colored coats, and no flowers to greet the weary wanderers with blushing smiles and refreshing fragrance.

Without the Light among men there might be a stoical righteousness, but no love to neighbor as to self, kindness to the weak would be unknown, missions of mercy to far off lands undreamed of, school-houses would be few and hospitals and asylums fewer still; there would be no cradle songs to close infant eyes, and music if made at all would be to incite the savage heart to war, or celebrate the defeat of adjoining tribes.

3. He furthermore gives power to bear and dare. He vitalizes, illumines and energizes every faculty and function; and transforms a fickle Simon into a

Rock, whom the threats of a synagogue could not move. For the God of Israel giveth strength and power unto His people. Daniel says, when there was no strength in him, and breath had left him, then there came again and touched him One like the appearance of a man, and He strengthened him and said, "O man greatly beloved, fear not; peace be unto thee; be strong, yea, be strong. And I was strengthened, and said, Thou hast strengthened me." When God touched the sons of Gad, men of the wilderness and men of might, the least was equal to a hundred and the greatest equal to a thousand. For they that stand ready and obedient in His presence shall change their weakness for His strength; they shall mount up with wings as eagles; they shall run, and not be weary; and they shall walk, and not faint. This sentence, dropped from the lips of an unknown speaker, "The world has never yet seen what God can do with a man wholly possessed by God," is said to have changed the life of the most distinguished Christian worker of our age.

The simple condition of such transforming power is a surrendered life in living touch and communion with the Son of the living God; then,

> "Weak as you are you shall not faint,
> And fainting, shall not die;
> Jesus, the strength of every saint,
> Shall aid you from on high."

II. This Band is United in Purpose.

1. The best and most effective union demands, first, separation. This Band separated itself from the sons of Belial. Paul has in mind a similar thought when writing to the Corinthians, where he says, What concord or agreement hath Christ with Belial? Wherefore come out from among them, and be ye separate, saith the Lord, and touch not the unclean thing; and I will receive you, and will be a Father unto you, and ye shall be My sons and daughters. Some one said to a sincere child of God, "I would give the world if I had your faith," and he replied, "Well, that is just what it costs." To be influential in the world one must not conform to the world. Abraham out of Sodom had more influence in and over Sodom than Lot, who abode there. The Spirit of God must first separate Paul and Barnabas from among men, and then send them to the Gentiles. Without this definite and separating experience life will be feeble and effort powerless.

2. Separation for the purpose of isolation is ruin,

but separation for the purpose of combination is power. Charcoal, saltpetre and sulphur are quite harmless, but combined form gunpowder; and carbon, oxygen and hydrogen produce nito-glycerine. Christians are to be separated, and then formed into bands and an army, with Christ as Captain, going forth conquering and to conquer, with His banner over them—" Love." Wesley said, with a band of twelve, who hated nothing but sin, and loved the Lord only, he would convert the world. We need such bands in every church, with a motto over its entrance, "All at it, and always at it." Then would the Church be edified, and the Kingdom of our Lord extended.

3. The bond of this band is Love, which is the bond of perfectness. In an age when all are tempted to seek their own, and not the things of Jesus Christ, love is needed to melt the hardness and the coldness, and drive away the bitterness, and fuse into an irresistible and irrepressible band; and when God touches hearts love to one another and Him will follow, for He is Love, and first loved us. "One touch of nature makes the whole world kin." One touch of Jesus Christ makes all men brothers. It is said that Lincoln's favorite verse was this:

> I live for those who love me,
> For those who know me true,
> For the Heaven that smiles above me
>   And awaits my coming to,
> For the cause that needs assistance,
> For the wrongs that need resistance,
> For the future in the distance,
>   For the good that I can do."

Touched by the spirit of Jesus one can say with Him, when hated and persecuted, "Father, forgive them; for they know not what they do," and with Paul, "I am made all things to all men that by all means I might save some." This is the purpose of every godly band and Jesus is the power and bond, and every member a bound-servant to Him.

III. This band was progressive in spirit, because it went with Him.

1. In harmony with Him: they as Enoch before, walked with Him in the same direction, having the same tendencies, the same object and purpose. His Word will not be searched for texts to sanction questionable conduct, nor will He be petitioned in prayer to bless selfish schemes, but His Word will be read and He himself will be sought to find the way, and the spirit in which they should walk. They pray not that He might meet with them, but that they might move with Him, while He is march-

ing on; and that He, and He through them may cast shadows of healing on the hopeless, and give hope to the helpless.

2. This daily walking by our Savour's side will beget Mutual Trust. Company and Captain may agree and move against a common enemy, yet there may be lacking mutual confidence and heart-harmony. On one occasion when the Jews saw the miracles Jesus did many believed in his name, but Jesus would not commit himself unto them, because he knew all men, and needed not that any should testify of man, because he knew what was in man. On the last Great-Day, when the angel Gabriel shall summon with his golden trumpet all the children of men for each to give an account of himself for the deeds done in the body; there will be many in that multitude to say, Lord, Lord, have we not prophesied in Thy name? cast out devils, and done many wonderful works? And Jesus will say, I never knew you as a member of the band whose heart God touched. One must possess as well as profess; one must have a godly character as well as a goodly name; God-likeness as well as the form of godliness. The lives of myriads are poor and puny, sunless and songless, because

Jesus could not trust His Word, His Spirit, Himself to them. Trust Him truly and He will trust you, " With a love that shall not die, till the sun grows cold, and the stars are old, and the leaves of the Judgment day unfold," and He will love you as He did the disciples unto the end.

3. And lastly, the band of men and women whose hearts Jesus touches, purifies and inspires, must keep step with Him, and must be content to take but one step at a time. Not ahead, as Peter was when he cut off Malchus' ear, nor behind, when he followed the Lord afar off, and denied Him. We, too, like Peter, are sometimes ahead of Jesus, and sometimes behind. Our feet are swift to run into evil, and slow on missions of mercy; the hands are quick to strike and tardy to give; the tongue of many is in haste to rob of reputation, to plunge a "dagger" into hearts, and divide homes, but slow to cheer and encourage the desponding and despairing; the eyes are quick to see, and even magnify motes into beams, but are to graces and virtues very blind. The only cure for going too fast or going too slow is walking with Jesus, belonging to the band whose body, soul and spirit God has touched, who possess Jesus, and are possessed by Him, and are willing to go into the

highway and hedges, and, with a love that never fails, compel men to come into an inheritance incorruptible, undefiled, and that fadeth not away.

And the pastor needs to stand by him, and uphold his hands, and to go with him, a band of men and women, whose hearts God has touched, and trained and inspired, who will lift burdens from breaking backs, wipe tears from weeping eyes, drive away sighing and sorrow from suffering saints, and pluck the pallor from pale cheeks, and clothe them with a smile.

The pastor, your pastor, needs in the future, as there has gone with him in the past, such a band to chase away the gloom of declining years, cheer his heart with the joy of your presence and personal work, prolong his days to bless your children as he has you, and crown his life with unfading flowers and fragrance, and make him rich in the jewels of ransomed souls.

[In the absence of Rev. M. J. Eckels, D. D., Pastor of the Arch Street Church, Philadelphia, who was providentially detained from coming to Carlisle for these anniversary services, Rev. George S. Chambers, D. D., Pastor of the Pine Street Church, Harrisburg, was called out from the audience, and made a very happy impromptu speech of congratulation. If he had been able to furnish a copy of his admirable address, it would have been printed in its place in these proceedings. Though prevented by sickness from appearing in person, Dr. Eckels has kindly furnished his address in manuscript, and it is presented herewith.]

"THE COMPARATIVE ADVANTAGES OF COUNTRY AND CITY PASTORATES."

BY

REV. MERVIN J. ECKELS, D. D.

GOOD PEOPLE OF THE SECOND PRESBYTERIAN CHURCH OF CARLISLE:—I appear among you on this happy occasion as one of the "Sons of this Church," and the son of one whom you all honored as an Elder of this congregation for many years. Having been invited to speak to you, I chose this topic, not so much because of "what I know" about city and country pastorates generally—although I should know something by experience, having spent eleven years in the pastorate in country or town churches, and five years of pastoral service in the heart of a great city—but I chose this topic because it was suggested by the experience of our beloved pastor of thirty years, whom we meet to honor to-day. Thirty years ago he came to this quiet country town, and began his ministry among us. The whole land was then before him as a young man. Some of us will remember how frequently, in his earlier ministry, our pastor was invited to preach in city pulpits, and what complimentary things were said about him on those occasions.

I am sure he could not contradict me if I should say, that in those days the doors of some very desirable city churches seemed ready to open at the touch of his friends, had he so much as " winked at" it. Dr. Norcross chose to abide in the country, and feed his flock, which scattered far and wide over these fertile fields of our peaceful valley. I have often wondered at this; for, though, like myself, country-bred, he seemed to me possessed of all the tastes and habits of a city man. Our pastor has ever been a lover of libraries and assemblies of "the brethren," such as abound in the city. To-day, as we meet to review these thirty years, I find myself wondering whether he could have been more useful or more happy in a city pastorate than here in Carlisle. As to some things, I can only speculate; as to other matters, experience enables me to speak with confidence.

I am persuaded that had he gone early to the city, he could scarcely have become the ripe scholar that he is to-day. The scholar is nourished, not so much by the great public libraries as by his own well selected library. I am confident that few Presbyterian pastors in Philadelphia to-day possess such a library as hides the walls of the study in our Manse in Carlisle. If they do own so many of the best books, they have not been able to read them as he has. The scholar needs not only books, but quiet hours—protracted, undisturbed periods for thought. This is almost impossible in a great city, where a prominent pastor is subject—not only to the demands of his own people, but of a great public, ever bent on robbing him of the time that belongs to his own congregation. "By their fruits ye shall know them." What Presbyterian pastor in the city of Philadelphia—save Dr. McCook, who is simply a "wonder" as a worker—has, during these thirty years, put into permanent form so many addresses and chapters of history as our pastor? To the Church at large, I am sure he has been more useful in the country than he could have been in the city pastorate.

Perhaps there is another reason why our country pastor has always been a scholarly preacher. Lyman Abbott, early in his pastorate in Plymouth Church, where he had surprised himself as well as his people by developing into a popular speaker, told them that they, by their manner of hearing, had made him what he had become. So I may say of the people of this Second Presbyterian Church of Carlisle. This is a "College town." The place has a traditional love of learning. I know that the average man and woman of this congregation—as I knew it, twenty-five years ago—did more reading and thinking on historical, philosophical and theological subjects, than the average man and woman as I know them in our city churches to-day. They had more time and, perhaps, more taste for it. Great commercial and social centres may be conducive to "high living," but not to "high thinking."

Perhaps our pastor is what he is, as a preacher, because his people have made him so.

Concerning another thing I am quite sure, Dr. Norcross, as a city pastor, could not have known his people, or been known by them, as he has been in Carlisle. No man can know a congregation of a thousand people as he needs to know them. Even our lamented Dr. John Hall, of New York, a rare exception in this respect, could not do it. The amount of personal intercourse possible with each individual is, necessarily, too limited to permit intimate acquaintance with many. If I may be allowed to introduce personal experience, I would simply refer to the fact, that, when pastor in a country town, it was my privilege to receive into the church, upon confession, scores of men. In my city pastorate the number of men thus received has been small in comparison. The difference in result has been chiefly due to the difficulty of securing personal intercourse with men, who can rarely be seen at home and never in their places of business without the presence of others. A city pastor is supposed to be well known, while a country pastor is regarded as obscure. On the contrary, any stranger coming into Carlisle might enquire for Dr. Norcross of any man whom he might chance to meet, with the assurance that he would be able to point him out; but you would enquire in vain for your speaker, in Philadelphia, except in the vicinity of his own church. And again, I may ask, how many of our city pastors are so well known throughout all the churches as our country pastor here in Carlisle?

Nevertheless, the city pastorate has its advantages. Whether a man can be as happy there as in the country will be determined by his personal tastes and habits. That he can be as useful, I fully believe. If he communes less with books and with nature, he comes more into contact with persons of all classes, and learns to adapt himself to an ever-changing environment. If in the country he can do more for a few persons; in the city he can do something to help more persons. He, if accessible, becomes a bureau of information to pastors seeking entrance to vacant pulpits, to a procession of young men and women seeking employment and companionship in our great city, to keepers of boarding-houses and those going to sojourn where they may find a place. There are more "lonely hearts to cherish" in the city than the country, more discouraged ones to be heartened and more "lost sheep of the house of Israel" to be gathered into the fold. The city pastor finds more opportunity to minister to those in Hospitals and Homes for the Aged and Friendless. The whole field of city missions and public charities lies about him, and, like his Master, he may constantly go about doing good. The conclusion of the whole matter is this: The best place for every pastor is where God wants him—whether in city or country. In this, too, we, who meet to greet and honor our pastor to-day, with true hearts that are loyal yet, after thirty years, are agreed; that we have wanted him and God has wanted him all these years in the country pastorate, in this good town of Carlisle, and this has been the best place for him.

"OUTLOOK OF THE CHURCH FOR THE TWENTIETH CENTURY."

BY

REV. SHELDON JACKSON, D. D., LL. D.

For the past two days we have been upon the mount of privilege. We have met in spirit with the noble men and women who, sixty-six years ago, established this Church, and their successors who have carried it forward so efficiently until the present. We have been encouraged by the united testimony of those who have spoken upon this occasion with regard to the sound orthodoxy that is the heritage of this people, and the liberality with which they have sought in the past to obey the divine command to "disciple" all nations, beginning at Jerusalem.

The missionary spirit, home and foreign, exhibited by this Church in its history is known throughout the earth, and I have no doubt the feeling in all hearts present is, that it is good to be here, and that, like Peter, James and John upon the Mount of Transfiguration, we would fain erect altars of thanksgiving and joy, and rest here from our labors. But this cannot be. The early disciples descended from the Mount of Transfiguration to meet their baffled associates, who could not heal the demoniac; and we likewise will pass from this mount of privilege and these days of special enjoyment to again take up our life-work, again to struggle with temptation and sin, and again engage in the battle of life. As doubtless the scene on the Mount of Transfiguration was a special preparation to Peter, James and John for their great prominence as "pillars in the Church" and leaders among the apostles; so we have in the good Providence of God been brought to this joyous occasion as a preparation for further work. We cannot live in the past; it is but a preparation for the future. The memory of past achievements should strengthen our faith to attempt still greater things for the Master.

The times in which we live demand more heroic living on the part of Christians; there has perhaps never been a time in the history of the world when there was so great unrest among all classes of people in all civilized lands; there has never been a period in the history of the world when great changes have been so rapid; when the demands of the Kingdom upon the children of God have been so great. The adult portion of this audience can remember when large portions of the earth were closed against the missionary, and the united prayer in Monthly Concert and in Christian homes and hearts was for an "open door." Then nation after nation was thrown open to the Gospel, and the cry went up for more men and women to enter the work. The men and women were supplied, and now the great cry of the Church should be for such a baptism of the Holy Spirit as will enable all Christians to recognize their stewardship so that the treasuries of the House of the Lord may be filled to overflowing, and thousands of men and women who are offering themselves for work can be sent. The orthodoxy of this Church in the past is a grand foundation for enlarged work in the future. Its well-known liberality in the past is but a training for Church-giving and greater consecration in the days to come—the preparation for better coming up to the help of the Lord in a time like this. We cannot without sin drop back; we cannot do less than in the past; we cannot remain where we are; we must go forward.

We stand before a future vast, momentous, appalling; vast in its possibilities, momentous in its opportunities, appalling in its results. As we face this unknown future, I do not wonder that the politician and the statesman shrink back; but I can not conceive how the Christian, with the promises of God behind him foreshadowing the complete triumph of good over evil, resting upon the everlasting arm for strength, and following where infinite wisdom leads should hesitate or hold back.

All progress is life, " expansion." When we cease to press forward, we do not simply stand still; we go back. To the Church of the Living God there is no going back—there is no standing still; if the Church is faithful to her divine Lord and Master she must press forward in both religious and civil matters. There must be ceaseless effort to purify the Government. Unflagging work to leaven the masses with Christianity; heroic attempts to take possession of the world for Christ. And if, in the Providence of God, lands are unexpectedly brought under our flag, it is simply an indication of the divine will that we are to have the protection of that flag, and its assistance in Christianizing and civilizing these populations unacquainted with our Christian civilization. It is to give us better vantage ground for Christian work.

At such a time not only the whole body of believers should press forward, but each individual church should realize more and more that they have been created and blessed for church work and church giving, and more fervent prayer for a day like this.

Let us then, with the opening of the new year and the commencement of a new period in the history of the life of this church, hail the future with joy, and "forgetting those things which are behind, and reaching forth unto those things which are before," let us "press toward the mark for the prize of the high calling of God in Christ Jesus." Let the one burning thought of our hearts day and night be the speedy triumph of the Redeemer's Kingdom. Let our own study and thought and prayer day by day be that we be found faithful in our places in securing this triumph. Let us see to it that thus we do our whole duty as good soldiers in Christ's army.

I congratulate you on the past, I bid you God speed for the future.

ADDRESSES.

Monday Evening, January 2, 1899.

DUNCAN M. GRAHAM, ESQ.,
PRESIDENT OF THE BOARD OF TRUSTEES,
PRESIDING.

MR. GRAHAM:

When the Chairman of the Committee of Arrangements informed me that I had been selected by the Committee to preside to-night, I felt keenly the honor conferred, but I felt it was not so much a personal compliment as a compliment intended for the lay side of the Church—to the Board, which I have the honor to represent, and to the Congregation at large, that it might be recognized on this joyous occasion.

Perhaps there was some desire on the part of the Committee to connect those of us who bear the burden and heat of the day with those worthies, of whom we heard so eloquently and ably yesterday, a venerated father having occupied for nearly thirty years the position, which the partiality of my fellow-members of the Board has conferred upon me; and I would be unfaithful to myself, unfaithful to the earnest convictions of my heart, did I not bring to-night to our Pastor, from the lay element of this church, the esteem and love of a loyal and united congregation.

Thirty years of ministerial life; three decades of human effort in the most exalted position that can come to man,—that is the occasion we are celebrating here to-night.

We of the laity are proud, modestly proud, of some things; we are proud of our Church organization; we are proud of our Church itself; we are proud of our educated ministry; we are humbly proud to think that, since its organization, the Presbyterian Church has been the bulwark against infidelity in all of its forms—at all times. The grosser forms of infidelity are easily met and vanquished, but the subtler forms of infidelity—those forms which require a cultivated intellect—and the strong cultured intellect of manly men to combat—have been met by the educated ministry of the Presbyterian Church and vanquished upon a hundred battlefields. We are proud of the part that our educated ministry took in the formation of the Constitution, which governs and controls this Union of States to-day. Yesterday we heard how the men of our church took part in the formation of that instrument; how it was modeled after the organization of the Presbyterian Church; how it has stood the storms and stress of time. It resisted the efforts of the contractionists in 1861, and under the Providence of God it will be equal to all the requirements of mistaken expansion in this the morning twilight of the Twentieth Century.

For the lay side of the Church, I may say this: I can say that the Pastor of this church has the loyalty and the devotion of a united people. I can say, furthermore, that there never was a time in the history of the Church when the Church was stronger and more able, nay more willing to contribute to all those charities, to all those boards which go to make up the active work of a Christian Church.

We are happy in this occasion; glad of the opportunity it gives us to say to our pastor and to the people of the Church that we are firmer and stronger in the faith. The learned gentleman who addressed you yesterday said that the past is secure. I say to you that the future is no less secure. To doubt the future is to discredit the thirty years of teaching of the man of God who has wrought so faithfully during all that time; it is to discredit the teachings of the fathers and the teachings of the mothers at whose knees we learned our prayers and our Shorter Catechism. We are ready now as our forefathers were to maintain the teachings of the Church in all their purity and in their strength. As I stand in this Church to-night, beneath this beautiful Gothic arch it seems symbolic of our faith; one span founded upon this Book, between which and us no mere man shall ever come; the other founded upon the right of private judgment, and that founded and bottomed upon an educated conscience, and meeting together at the top in beauty and grace, complete the arch of our royal Presbyterian faith. I believe that the young men of the Church will maintain it as strong and pure and beautiful as it was handed down to us by those who have gone before, and who rest in the shade of the trees on the other side.

And now our friends have come to-night to rejoice with us on this occasion. It has been stated by a learned writer that the first lawyer in a community should be and ought to be and generally is the first citizen of that community, and there is good reason in this. When he combines character and integrity and purity of life; when he has the respect and love and esteem of every one, one to whom the widow and orphan turn in time of deepest distress and woe, surely such a citizen is a blessing to any community. We have such a citizen with us tonight. He is of our faith, although not in our church, and I take pleasure in introducing to you one to whom your thoughts will instantly turn,— Judge Henderson.

HON. R. M. HENDERSON:

I thank you, Mr. Chairman, for your introduction. When I was first asked to be present upon this occasion, some five or ten minutes were allowed me. Subsequently it was kindly suggested that I might make a short speech. I assure you that I shall not trespass upon the time or patience of this audience, for I will keep within the limit first suggested—five or ten minutes.

I am here without exordium, and I have no apology to make, for I am a volunteer, not a regular. It is, however, with unfeigned pleasure that I arise to say a word upon this most interesting occasion—the anniversary of a pastorate of thirty years. Think of it—a full generation has come in and gone out before him whom we honor to-night. This at once brings into view the pulpit and the pew—the preacher and the people. We are told that this Church—the Second Presbyterian Church—is sixty-six years old, and that the present pastorate covers almost half of that period. How suggestive! Who has gone before? I recall the learned and scholarly McGill. The eloquent and incisive Moore. The quiet, patient, lovable, saint-like Johnston. To follow in the footsteps of these men of mark, and to hold the people down to the work inaugurated by them for so long a pastorate, is an honor that cannot be measured by any words of mine. I simply place upon his brow, " Well done."

But what of this congregation? Whence comes it? Your fathers and your mothers, now looking down upon this hallowed scene, point to the gray walls of the old First Church and proudly claim that as their first resting place in the pilgrimage of life here below.

But you tell me there has been a separation, and speak of the New School and the Old School. And this formed part of the historical discourse to which we listened with so much attention and profit. And now historically speaking, the line of demarkation has grown so thin, failing even to rest in the most vivid imagination, that it, like Mason and Dixon's line, has become a thing of the past. And your historian does not fail to tell us that it was only a finger point of Providence to a higher, broader and more enobling re-union of hearts and of hands in the Presbyterian fold. All to the glory of God!

There is one thing of significance, pointed out yesterday. When this people went out to new pastures, you left us the property, but you took all the money, and have been living on fat things ever since. I may say, however, you divided the *grace*. You did leave us the pastor and some of the sainted elders. I believe it was Dr. Sprole who said, or is reported to have said, of these noble men of the First Church, that there never would be peace in his church till one of his elders was in Heaven, and the other at Oberlin. We know that the one reached his destination upon earth, and grounded in the faith, we believe that the other was registered on High.

I congratulate you people of this congregation upon what has gone before, I congratulate you upon these days and upon this house, I congratulate you upon the strength and beauty of these walls. I congratulate you upon the manna which has sanctified your lives since you went out from the old First Church.

But I hear the cry, "Watchman, what of the night?" The morning cometh, the morning of opportunity, the morning of preparation; the morning of victory, for the enemy are without on hill and in valley thirsting for the blood of your people, your lands and your cattle. But fear not; led by your great Captain against the enemy, fighting under the King of Kings, when the night cometh, your banner will sweep over the ramparts.

But, my dear sir, I would be unjust to my own feelings if I failed to bow in reverence to your life-work here; your manhood in the pulpit, and in the community, ever abreast with reform, loved as a man, respected as a citizen. I congratulate you upon the possession of this people who sit at your feet and strew your pathway with flowers; this wall of separation between us—these flowering plants and beautiful evergreens which decorate this platform— is a loving tribute of true devotion from your people. I congratulate you upon days and months and years of

CONGRATULATIONS. 211

peace and joy and happiness among this people. But, ah, sir, your paths are not always strewed with roses. In all the wide range of humanity, if there is deep sorrow, it comes to the pastor of a loved and and loving people. The unbidden tear may dim the manly eye, for the dearest ties of affection have been sundered time and time again. Tears may furrow the blanched cheek. The pain of anguish may fill the heart of pastor and of people,——

But remember :

> "Brief life is here our portion,
> Brief sorrow, short lived care :
> The life that knows no ending—
> The tearless life is there."

MR. D. M. GRAHAM :

When we Presbyterians think of the founder of our faith, the great Calvin, our thoughts almost always turn to that other great Reformer, and almost cotemporary of Calvin, Luther, and we feel that the roses which clamber over the very low wall which divides us in doctrine shed their fragrance alike on Lutheran and Presbyterian. I have the honor to present to you Dr. Wile.

DR. H. B. WILE:

I very much appreciate the reference which the honored Chairman of this meeting has given to our great Reformer, Luther, in connection with your Calvin; and although I think that we may differ on some points of doctrine, nevertheless the little couplet comes to my mind which runs something like this:

> "We are not one, and yet not two,
> But look alike as sisters do."

When the good pastor of this church asked me to take a place on the programme this evening, according to his usual modesty, he suggested that what I might say should be very moderate, that I should not be at all extreme in my remarks of congratulation. The request reminded me of a story that is told of Dr. Bethune, whom some of you may have known.

He was asked on a certain occasion to officiate at the funeral services of a man who had been a member of the Society of Spiritualists. The wife of the man had been brought up a good, strict Presbyterian, but had finally been persuaded to go with her husband to his society. After his death, the brothers of the man who had died insisted that there should be no minister there. The widow, however, recalling the good training of her girlhood days, insisted upon having a Presbyterian minister, and Dr. Bethune was asked to conduct the services. The day after the funeral one of the brothers met the Doctor, and said, "Doctor, we didn't like that sermon that you preached yesterday." The Doctor said, " I am not surprised, sir, because I know your faith, and I can readily understand that you would not agree with what I said." " But," the brother added, " that is not all, I want to say ; the widow is not any better pleased with the sermon." " Well," said the Doctor, " I can't help even that ; if I were asked to do the same thing again, I am sure I would talk in the same way." Then in a storm of indignation he said, " That is not the worst, sir ; last night we called up the spirit of our departed brother, and he said that he was not at all pleased with your sermon." " Why," said the Doctor, " the impudent fellow ! I have been preaching funeral sermons for fifty years, and that is the first corpse that has ever had the audacity to speak back at me." Now, I am somewhat in the same situation. I am very much afraid that if my congratulation does not suit Dr. Norcross, he may speak back at me.

The greatest compliment that can be given to any

minister of the Gospel can certainly be given to Dr. Norcross, and that is, that he preaches Jesus Christ. To be good, and to be constantly trying to make others good, to be giving one's whole life-work in trying to make men perfect in Christ Jesus, is the highest ideal of the ministry, and I feel assured that Dr. Norcross has been doing that here among you for the past thirty years.

Not very long ago I heard of a man who happened to become the pastor of a very prominent church in Chicago, and after being there a short time, he gave evidence that he was not orthodox, and so was dismissed from the congregation. A few years later he happened to be in Chicago over Sunday, and asked the privilege to preach once more to these people, whom he had served in former years. The pastor of the church, knowing the man and his creed, hesitated, and finally, though with great reluctance, consented. The church was crowded to the doors. For one hour the man denounced the idea of the necessity of an atonement, and ridiculed the need of a Saviour. The pastor of the church waited patiently till he was through, and then, without a word of comment, he turned to the congregation and announced the 249th Hymn. The great organ commenced fairly to throb as if her pipes knew what it all meant. Stop after stop was added, as if the organist realized that even the great organ could not quite do itself justice. Then the whole congregation rose to its feet, and every man, woman and child joined in the service, and with a fervor such as they had never known before, sang:

> "All hail the power of Jesus' name,
> Let angels prostrate fall;
> Bring forth the royal diadem,
> And crown Him Lord of all."

It was enough of a rebuke. They gave evidence that they still believed in the Lord Jesus Christ. I feel very confident that if you should ever be so unfortunate as to have such preaching as that, you as a congregation would be so well instructed that you would at once be aroused, and expel from your pulpit the man who would not follow after the blessed Christ, whom Dr. Norcross has preached to you so faithfully for the past thirty years.

Dr. Norcross, I congratulate you. I congratulate you that these good people have recognized your true worth; that they have recognized the character of the preaching which you have done for these many years, and have ever been glad to uphold you and co-operate with you and love you. My dear friends, I congratulate you as members of the Second Presbyterian Church of Carlisle, that for thirty years Dr. Norcross has been willing to stay with you, and has been able to endure you, for I am sure that in his estimation there is no other congregation quite as nice and quite as desirable as this congregation which he has learned to love so dearly.

A few months ago in New York City, when our "boys in blue" came back from the scenes of war, the whole city was out to meet them. Great throngs lined the entire route from the Battery to the Armory. You remember that as soon as the men touched our shores, the bands played "The Star Spangled Banner" and the chimes on old Trinity sang out "Home Sweet Home" and the great mass of human beings, the great mass of eager, anxious, loving hearts that had gathered about the Armory, sang,

> "Praise God, from whom all blessings flow,
> Praise Him, all creatures here below:
> Praise Him, above, ye heavenly host,
> Praise Father, Son, and Holy Ghost."

That is about what you people have been doing for these two days, and you have great reason for gratitude and thanksgiving. To-night you are praising God, from whom all blessings flow, because He has watched over you and blessed you so abundantly as pastor and people.

Dr. Norcross, again I congratulate you, and pray very sincerely that when your course is run, and the goal is reached, you may have sparkling in your crown many precious souls whom you have led by the aid of the Holy Spirit to our blessed Lord.

MR. D. M. GRAHAM:

If I were to ask Dr. Norcross to-night who, amongst the pastors of the town, had been his strongest ally in his warfare against that old common enemy we heard of in one of the sermons of yesterday, I am sure that he would speak the name of one who is here to-night, one who is strong in disputation and able in polemics, yet possesses all the lovely graces of character that make up the ideal pastor and Christian gentleman. I present to you Dr. Frysinger.

DR. W. M. FRYSINGER:

When I came to Carlisle in the Spring of 1870 to take charge of what was then the Emory Church, I found here as genial and scholarly a body of preachers as I have ever had the good fortune to meet with. Dr. Wing was then pastor of the First Presbyterian Church. A man as firm as a rock in principle, and yet as gentle as a woman in manner. I do not think that it detracts in the least from the nobleness of his character to say that he was one of the most motherly men I have ever known. Dr. Swartz was Pastor of the First Lutheran Church; a man whose voice was music and whose speech was poetry. Dr. Foulk was pastor of the Reformed Church; a solid, sensible, good man. He was my next door neighbor, and he was very fond of gardening. The fence between our lots was as low as the denominational fence between us, and he would now and then hand me over a bunch of his famous celery, and at the same time some of his practical remarks, as acceptable and as palatable as this luscious vegetable, which expressions I would store up and often use in some of my own sermons.

I learned a great deal from Dr. Norcross also in those days. He preceded me by about two years, and we were the youngest pastors in the city at that time, and I think he feels as I do that we are the two youngest pastors in the town now. Under the imperative rule of our Church, I was compelled to leave this pleasant community at the end of three years, and it was twenty-one years more before I returned to take charge of the Allison Memorial Church. In this interval, I filled four different positions, which, with my first and present term of service in Carlisle, makes six terms of service, during all of which Dr. Norcross has remained with these same people at this same Church. As a loyal Methodist, subscribing to the polity of our Church, which prescribes an itinerant ministry, I am placed in an anomalous position this evening, as I presume I am expected to congratulate Dr. Norcross and his people on the advantages of a settled pastorate, nevertheless I can do this conscientiously and heartily.

Each system has its advantages and disadvantages. "John," said the country mother to her boy, who had made up his mind to leave the old farm and go out into the great world and seek his own fortune, "a rolling stone gathers no moss." "Yes, mother, that is true," replied the boy, "but a setting hen lays no eggs." I am just now confronted with the fact that in three months I must leave my present field of labor and go out like Abraham "not knowing whither," and I confess a settled pastorate would have at this time some charms for me.

In a lengthy term of service such as your Pastor has rendered here, I recognize some great advantages. One is, that it compels a minister to be on his good behavior; he must necessarily be an example for both believers and unbelievers, for the eyes of the entire community are upon him. He must pray very earnestly and faithfully while so many are doing the watching, and must walk as he prays. Of all men, a pastor must walk most circumspectly. A brother of my own Conference was once an innocent illustration of this. Screams were heard coming from the parsonage, and a number of persons rushed to a window and looked in. To their surprise they beheld his wife running about the room, while he was striking at her excitedly with a cane. Although this couple were as amiable and affectionate as any married pair I have ever known, it took them months to convince their congregation and community that the husband was not a wife-beater, but in this instance was heroically trying to kill a mouse which had taken refuge in the folds of the lady's dress. Dr. Norcross, should one of these dreadful animals ever attack your good lady, take my advice,—do not run for your cane, but run after the members of your Session, and call them in for her protection, and thus save your own reputation.

Seriously, I congratulate you, Doctor, on having gone in and out before this community all these years, and sustained an unblemished reputation. It is a great moral achievement for a minister, under the trying events of ministerial life, to be looked upon as above reproach for so long a time, and to maintain the appreciation and good-will of a congregation like this. I see another great advantage in so long a pastorate, in that it compels a minister to do his best. We Methodist ministers, being compelled to go from one place to another, can preach our famous sermon on "Simon's wife's mother lay sick of a fever" as often as we move, without complaint from our hearers; but if a settled pastor were to venture upon as many diagnoses of this celebrated case, it would not be long before both subject and preacher would be put in quarantine. I am about concluding a term of five years of service, and in that time my people have heard five hundred sermons or more; but when I recall the brain-sweat these sermons have cost me, and the nervous chills that they have given me in their delivery, I stand aghast at the thought that during thirty years these solemn talks would be modified just six-fold; and as I look at Dr. Norcross, and think he has gone through all this, I feel like repeating the first line of the hymn which we sang at our New Year service yesterday, "And are we yet alive, and see each other's face?"

I congratulate you, Doctor, that you have endured all this, and yet preach with a freshness and vigor which cause you to be in greater demand for special occasions than ever. In twenty-one years from now I hope to come back to Carlisle again (that is the nearest I can calculate it according to the orbit in which I have been moving), and I expect to see Dr. Norcross looking just as hale and hearty as he does now, and find him preaching with just as much vigor as ever. Should I not be so fortunate as to return to Carlisle again, I have "good hope through grace," which is a Methodist as well as a Presbyterian phrase, to get to a better place than Carlisle, and, Doctor, let me say in Methodist parlance,

"If I get there before you do,
I'll shout to see you coming too."

You will find me in the New Jerusalem, on the corner of Hallelujah street and Glory avenue, and when you come along, walk right in, without knocking, and while my wife accompanies us on her golden harp, we will sing, "We'll never say good-bye."

MR. D. M. GRAHAM:

Sixty-six years ago our fathers left the old homestead over on the Square, and started out to make a new home for themselves. In their new home they grew and prospered, but the love and esteem they had for the old place never left them, nor their children. We are one in the faith in which we believe; we may be "distinct as the billows," yet we are "one as the sea." The memories of those who established the Presbyterian faith in the Cumberland Valley, in the old Church on the Square, are just as dear to us as to those who remain in the old homestead, and the names of Steele and Duffield, Nisbet and Davidson, and the saintly Dr. Wing are part of our heritage, of which we are truly proud.

The pastor of the old homestead, of the old Church, is here to-night, and we shall be glad to hear from Mr. Hagerty.

REV. A. N. HAGERTY.

MY DEAR BROTHER:—We are here to extend our congratulations to you, this evening, not because you have lived so long, as pastor of this church, but that you have lived so well. The life of the pastor of a great congregation, like this one, over which you have so graciously and successfully presided, during this long period of happy years, is not measured by time, but by deeds. A person may occupy a great deal of space or time in this world, only to waste it. Such has not been the record of your life during these years. As the Apostle John commends Demetrius, "There is good testimony from every one, and from the church, and from the truth itself," (3 John, 12. Syriac V.); so do we commend you.

This church, with its splendid history, standing for the Truth immovable, zealous for the spread of the Gospel in every mission field of the world, is your imperishable monument. It will "give good testimony" to you and your work, while it remains "one stone upon another."

But it is the Truth, the Word, the Christ, mirrored in your own life, that "sounds forth" your praises this night. After all has been weighed, man is the "greatest thing in the world." For man the Church is in the world. While the ultimate and supreme purpose of the Church is the glory of God, yet her direct and immediate reason for existence is the redemption of lost man. Within her walls man is to be redeemed by the Blood of Christ, completed in Him, for the "Everlasting Habitations." It is when the Apostle of Love sees in Demetrius as in a mirror one walking like unto the Son of Man, that he holds him in the very highest esteem.

So, My Dear Brother, as these people of this church and community have seen in you, as you walked among them, the living Christ manifested, have they held you in all honor.

But, sir, while we gather here to congratulate you, and bestow upon you the fullest measure of credit due you for the splendid work you have been permitted to accomplish as the Lord's minister to this people, yet we cannot lay all the crowns at your feet, nor would you accept such a tender.

There is a great deal in blood. In fact, the divine word says that, "In the blood is the life." This Church is of noble ancestry. Great things were doubtless expected of you by the worthy fathers who sent forth this nursling congregation. They gave you a good dowery, and expected you to keep the blood clean. That you should have kept it up to the standard is greatly to your credit.

To change the figure. As the stream cannot rise higher than the fountain, neither did the Old Stone First expect that you would be greater than you have been. Nobly have you done your work. A "Good man, full of the Holy Ghost," stood at the altar when you were consecrated and sent forth, and of that same Spirit you have grown rich in good works, and strong in numbers and resources.

We felicitate you on the occurrence of this happy event. To both pastor and people we bear the hearty congratulations of the Old Mother Church, and devoutly pray that you may long be spared in efficient labors for our common Lord and Master.

MR. D. M. GRAHAM:

One hundred and sixty-six years ago there came into the Cumberland Valley a set of men, sturdy, manly men, driven from home, in search of that liberty which was denied them there. They were Scotch Highlanders and Scotch Lowlanders; they had stayed for a short time in the north of Ireland, hence the term "Scotch-Irishmen;" they came on and up into the Cumberland Valley; they brought with them that love of home, that love of learning, that love of God, which all the bloody dragoons of Claverhouse could not take from them. They founded schools; they built churches; and believing in an educated ministry, they founded Dickinson College. It prospered for a time, and then for reasons which I need not state here to-night, that institution was turned over to a strong sister denomination, under which it has flourished and grown strong and powerful.

Our interest as a Church in the old College has never waned or lessened, and the noblest and most beautiful specimen of architecture that adorns the old campus is a gift of a member of this church, in memory of a devoted husband and father; and the ground upon which the beautiful Denny Hall stands, which has just been completed through the energy and effort of the present head of the institution, was donated by a Presbyterian family. Therefore, our interest in the old institution is still as strong as ever, and we are glad and proud of the fact that it has grown in strength and might and power, although we regret that it is no longer a Presbyterian institution. We have with us to-night the head of that institution, and we shall be glad indeed to hear from the able and scholarly President, Dr. Reed.

DR. GEO. EDWARD REED:

Mr. Chairman, Ladies and Gentlemen:—It is a very great pleasure for me to respond to the kind invitation of the committee having in hand the arrangement for this anniversary, and to join with the many friends of our honored brother, the Rev. Dr. Norcross, in hearty congratulations on the auspicious event now being commemorated. I am to speak, as I understand, in the first place as the representative of the old college in whose fortunes our Presbyterian friends have taken such great interest in the hundred and more years of its eventful history.

Speaking for the college, I cannot forget its deep obligations to those men of Presbyterian stock who were interested in its foundation and early development during the first seventy or eighty years of its eventful history. It is a great thing in this world to be well born, and that Dickinson was well born, of course, goes without saying; for as you all know, it had its origin very largely under Presbyterian auspices. Up to 1833 it was very largely under Presbyterian control, and during the years of its subsequent history the kind feeling of the Presbyterians of the country toward the old college has undergone no change. Very much of its material growth, as your honored President has intimated, has come to us through Presbyterian channels; and as gratitude has been defined as "a lively expectation of favors to come," we beg you all to believe that we are most sincerely and profoundly grateful for the favors which have been received—a clear intimation of our large expectations of our Presbyterian friends for the coming years.

It is a matter for congratulation that the students of Dickinson College have had the opportunity during so many years of hearing not only the men of the religious body under whose general auspices the college now exists, but also the discourses of the able and distinguished men who have filled the pulpits of the churches of Carlisle. The requirement of Dickinson is that each student shall attend the church which he may elect as his church home once upon each Sabbath. They have full liberty of election, and are privileged to attend the services of churches other than those elected during the remaining portion of the day. Some of them keep this regulation, it is true, in the spirit far more than in the letter. But the large numbers in attendance at the various churches of the city attest the attractive power of the many able men who adorn the pulpits of the town of Carlisle. I am sure that Dr. Norcross has, during all these years, seen very many of the students of the college in attendance upon the services of this church; and I, as the President, have had profound satisfaction in the fact that the opportunity of hearing so able and earnest and accomplished a minister of the Word as is Dr. Norcross has been the privilege of our young men. Quite a large number of our students also have been Presbyterians in faith, and members of this Church, and from these I have heard frequent expressions of the deep and abiding interest taken by Dr. Norcross in their welfare. The services of Dr. Norcross have been of invaluable assistance to hundreds of our men. So, on behalf of the old college, I desire to congratulate this eminent minister of the Gospel upon the successful completion of thirty years of ardent service, and to wish him a fervent God-speed for years to come.

Having now spoken briefly from the standpoint of the college, allow me, in conclusion, to say a word for myself. Sitting here to-night and listening to the continued eulogies pronounced upon my eminent brother, I have been asking myself, "How is Dr. Norcross feeling under all this outflow of appreciation, all these expressions of congratulation, of esteem and of respect?" He must, I am sure, feel very proud and I feel like saying to him, as my good mother used to say to me so frequently—indeed, almost every day of the week: "George, I hope that my boy will keep humble." I am sure that Mrs. Norcross to-night and for many days to come will have to say to her excellent husband, "George be sure that you keep humble." Still, for all that has been said about you, my dear Doctor, I fear that she must feel even prouder than yourself, and so perhaps the best advice that I can give is, be sure that both of you keep humble.

We have been hearing a great deal about Dr. Norcross. Very much as to his character as a citizen, his standing as a man, his orthodoxy of doctrine, his wonderful success as the expounder of Scripture, of the vigorous way in which he contends for the faith once delivered to the saints; so much, indeed, that I have been wondering if anything would remain for me to say when my turn to speak should come. One thought came to me which perhaps is my salvation. During all these anniversary services Dr. Norcross has been the continual theme; as if there were no one remaining worthy of mention in connection with his work. But, my dear Doctor, it occurs to me, that in all this outflow of good feeling they have ignored the person who more than any other has made your success possible, who has been back of all your triumphs and without whose smiles and zeal, companionship and co-operation, you would not have accomplished one-half of what you have been able to accomplish. By your side sits a beautiful, modest and accomplished woman—the woman who has practically made you, and still, so far as I know, not one word has been said about her—the woman whom everybody loves and esteems. What would you have been without her, the constant sharer of your joys and your stay and abiding support? All must have been impressed by the remarkable neatness of the Doctor's appearance. Always he looks as though fresh from the hands of his tailor. Whoever saw him when he was not as it were "spick and span." How many have stopped to reflect that he poses before his wife and passes the ordeal of her examination before he appears in public!

Again, he has been preaching sermons here for thirty years. Think of it! Two sermons a day for thirty years. But did you ever stop to think that for Mrs. Norcross there has practically been two sermons every Sabbath for sixty years? Do you not know that every sermon that the Doctor has preached has been rehearsed before Mrs. Norcross prior to its public delivery, and that she has been compelled to hear them twice over each week? Sixty years of preaching for her from Dr. Norcross, while you have had but thirty, and still no gray hairs are visible. All hail and all honor to the pastor's wife, beloved by every one in Carlisle privileged with her acquaintance. Seriously speaking, it is in the power of the pastor's wife ordinarily to make or unmake him so far as his success is concerned. No duty, therefore, can be more important than for a man intending the pastorate, to select a competent and helpful companion. Dr. Norcross, allow me, therefore, to say with all sincerity and truth—and in uttering the words I am sure I am but expressing the sentiments of hundreds of people who have known her during these years, and loved her—that much of your success as a minister of the Gospel of Jesus Christ has been due to your noble and effective help-mate. May God's blessing be upon you both, therefore, and may you long be comrades, to work together for the glory and honor of our common Lord and Master, Jesus Christ.

I remember hearing the late William Evarts tell of a woman who, at thirty years of age, married a man of sixty. A friend, calling upon her a short time after the wedding, found the lady dissolved in tears. "Are you unhappy?" said the friend. "Very unhappy, indeed," was the reply. "Has your husband been unkind to you?" "No, no man could be kinder." "Have you had any differences, such as are common sometimes between husbands and wives?" "There has never been the slightest unpleasantness between us." "Then, why do you appear to be so distressed? What are you worrying about?" "Well, you must remember that I am thirty years of age and he is sixty, and while that is all right now, I am worrying myself to death when I think that when I will be sixty he will be one hundred and twenty." That is what has been worrying me. I have been thinking that Dr. Norcross has officiated in this Church for thirty years, and you have not had any candidate for this Church for thirty years, and consequently, you do not know the pleasure there is in selecting a candidate. I am thinking what on earth will become of you after Dr.

CONGRATULATIONS.

Norcross has celebrated his sixtieth anniversary, and you have to go a-candidating. Some time ago, in a neighboring Presbyterian Church, a committee was appointed to select a new pastor. Time elapsed, and the congregation desired information as to how the committee were succeeding in their task. Finally, the following report was read, and I had the pleasure of doing the reading: " Your committee begs to report that during a period of nine months we have heard and examined seventy-five men. We have not made any selection yet, but we are hoping that in a few weeks we shall be able to report to you that we have selected a man who will possess all the qualities which the various members of this congregation have intimated to us they desire their future pastor to possess." When we think that in that case seventy-five men were examined, how many will have to be examined, Doctor, to fill your place when it shall become vacant?

I am rejoiced that for thirty years we have had in the pulpit of this noble church a man of broadest scholarship, of largest humanity, of profound and reverent faith, one familiar with all the questions and shifting opinions of the age, one who has not hesitated to examine very thoroughly every theory which has been propounded, but who has in all the storms of skepticism which have swept over the Church, stood loyally and squarely by the Word of God, and by the principles of that glorious faith, of which he was the consecrated defender.

I must not delay you longer. There are other speakers upon this programme. May the teachings of this noble minister of God reach the hearts of all! May the fires of piety and of pure devotion to God and His truth ever burn brightly upon the Presbyterian altar, and may the gracious blessing of God the Father, the Son and the Holy Ghost rest upon this eminent and accomplished minister of the Word and upon his devoted and loving wife!

MR. D. M. GRAHAM:

We have with us to-night one of the descendants of that Scotch-Irish race, whose name indicates his birth and descent. We shall be glad indeed to hear from Rev. McClean to-night. I see him sitting in the audience before me.

REV. R. F. McCLEAN:

After sitting here for almost two hours, I shall add but few words to the many eulogies and congratulations that you have already heard, and nothing but the sense of gratitude and friendship would lead me to thrust myself upon you now. A year after your pastor came to you, I made his acquaintance under rather trying circumstances, for I was to be subjected at his hands to a severe though kindly examination in Greek preparatory to being received as a candidate for the ministry. Ever since that time until now I can testify to his kindly and unfaltering friendship. In the early days he was a brother to us, and we always felt that we had his sympathy. It was from his lips and on this consecrated spot that I received with the lamented Green—who spent his saintly life in Japan—the solemn charge at our ordination.

Dr. Norcross was helpful to us from our admission into the ministry, and I can corroborate emphatically all that has been said of his ability and faithfulness as a pastor, of the faithfulness with which he has preached the word of God and the Gospel of Jesus Christ; for it has been my privilege at two periods, with my family, to be members of his congregation, and during the latter period, extending about a year and a half, he has been our friend indeed. From this pulpit we not only get the Presbyterian doctrines stated in modest but emphatic terms, but we hear the word of God in its fullest degree, and the gratefulness which I feel for him wells up from the depth of my heart.

The faithfulness of this pastor can not be questioned; he has not only endeared himself to this congregation but to the people of this community. Not only have the cultured heard him gladly, but our little children have received from his hands the Word of God in its plainest terms. That is a subject of eulogium. The success of this long pastorate has been due to his labor and fidelity to the welfare of the Church. We know that he has had the happiness of his people at heart, and for them we believe he will devote his best efforts in the years to come, for they are people worthy of their pastor. We have felt it a privilege to have been a part of this congregation, and we have received many tokens of kindness at the hands of our beloved pastor, and our hearts' best wish and earnest prayer is for a continuation of this union that has so successfully lasted for thirty years.

MR. D. M. GRAHAM:

It has been the pride of Dr. Norcross' ministry of thirty years that eight of his boys have gone into the ministry of the Church. One of these boys is here to-night. We shall be glad to hear from Rev. George Bucher.

REV. GEORGE BUCHER:

It is a pleasure for me, Doctor, to add my congratulations to the many words of eulogium of the gentlemen who have gone before me. I can endorse every word of congratulation that has been tendered here to our beloved pastor. It is a great pleasure for me to be here to-night, and to bear testimony to the wonderful work and to the patient kindness of my pastor and my friend. Something has been mentioned, I believe, about the boys who have gone out from this church in the ministry, who have taken up the work of Jesus Christ, to preach the glorious Gospel of the Son of God to the world. I belong to that group. I am one of the boys of this church, and I feel proud that I can be here to represent the boys who are not so fortunate as I am in being present. My connection with this Church only dates from the time I came to live in Carlisle, but my connection with this congregation is in one sense far longer. I can go back not only to my father, but to my grandfather*, who, when a student in Dickin-

---

*Dr. Robert G. Young, for many years an Elder in the Presbyterian Church at Mechanicsburg, Pa.

son College, was with this Church, and took an active part in its early history. I can therefore offer my beloved pastor our congratulations, because I stand as it were in a special relation to this Church.

Perhaps there is another reason that I have been selected by the boys to offer our congratulations to our pastor, and that is, all these boys have gone out from Carlisle into the world preaching the Gospel, and enforcing the doctrines that they were taught in this Church. I have been compelled to come two thousand miles to be here, and I am very glad to be here to participate in these glorious exercises, and to say to our beloved pastor that it is my privilege and my pleasure to tender to him the congratulations of his boys; to tender to you our thanks, and to give you some evidence of our appreciation. Therefore, to you, to your loving wife, and to your family, we give our hearty thanks for the many kind things you have done in our behalf.

And now, finally, let me say, I feel so proud, as I stand here, that I received my interpretation of the Gospel of Jesus Christ from Dr. Norcross; I feel proud that I have been here to see our pastor complete his thirty years of noble service in this church, and may God bless him, his home and his family, and keep him here for many years to come, in order that he may continue in his noble work as a minister of Jesus Christ, and a faithful pastor of this beloved Church.

MR. D. M. GRAHAM:

Our pastor wishes to say a word for himself, and we are always glad to hear him.

DR. NORCROSS:

I shall not trust myself to say all that is in my heart to-night, but I must say at least, I thank you! Words are very inadequate things at such a time as this. I am truly grateful to you all for helping to celebrate this anniversary, which means so much to both pastor and people.

I said the other day to a friend that I had never been called to a field I wanted. I have had three charges, and I did not desire any of them. I went out to my first charge, not that I wanted it, but because the Lord opened the way for me to begin work there. I was called to a much smaller church from my first one, and at a little more than half the salary. I did not want to go, but my brethren of the Presbytery voted that I should go, and so I went

I wondered for a long time what the Lord intended by that change, but when I found my wife in that charge, then I knew. You do not know, and can never know, what a blessing that wife has been to me.

I was invited to visit this field, and twice declined to come. When the invitation came the third time, I thought the Lord was in it, and I came, and it resulted in my settlement here. At first I was homesick, and longed to go back to the West, but I soon found that there was a great work to do, and I became interested and happy as the work opened up before me, and so here I have remained all these years.

Some one has said that a long pastorate requires much mutual patience between pastor and people. Well, the people have been very patient with me, but I have never felt myself very much tried with them. They have always been kind to me; and I am sure I have been as happy here as I could have been anywhere.

As to the place where we shall work, it seems to me, we may well leave that to the will of the Lord. Our old college President once said in my hearing, "If we commit our way unto the Lord, He will guide us as certainly as though a pillar of cloud went before us by day and a pillar of fire by night." I think it is true, and though he leads us by a way we know not, it proves in the end the right way. God only knows how I love this church, and God only knows how hard it would be for me to leave it; and yet, I am sure, if it were the Lord's will for me to do so, there would be something better in store for me some where, and I could trust Him. I think as we grow older we find how faithfully He leads, and how surely we can trust Him. He always takes care of His people, and if we put ourselves into His kind care and keeping, we shall be cared for.

Once more, I want to thank you all, dear friends, for all the graceful and gracious words you have spoken here during these anniversary services. I hope I shall not be unduly exalted by what you have said. I know my own failures too well to be flattered. I know I am only a poor sinner saved by grace. I am not so foolish as to believe that it is anything but the kindness of your hearts, and your love for me personally, that has inspired all your kind congratulations. May God bless you all, and reward you a thousand-fold for all your kindness to me and mine!

Mr. D. M. GRAHAM:

And now, I wish on behalf of the ladies of the congregation—God bless them!—to extend a cordial invitation to you all, every one here, I except none, to come with us to the church parlors, and we will try to make it pleasant for you. They have prepared a collation, and we wish to extend to our beloved pastor and his good wife our best congratulations, and I ask you all to come with us and we will try and make you glad.

THE RECEPTION.

Immediately after the conclusion of the exercises in the church a most delightful reception was tendered Dr. and Mrs. Norcross in the church parlors under the auspices of the ladies of the congregation. The receiving party was composed of Dr. and Mrs. Norcross, Rev. Sheldon Jackson, D. D., and wife, and the Elders of the church and their wives. It seemed as if the entire membership of the church was present to extend to their beloved pastor and his esteemed wife the most cordial assurances of their personal affection and regard. Not only was

THE RECEPTION.

the church fully represented, but a large number of the membership of other churches in the community and those outside of any church connection were present to extend their hearty congratulations. It was indeed a most joyous and happy occasion and the warmth and heartiness of the spirit manifested by all showed how deep and sincere is the regard entertained for Dr. Norcross not only by his own people but by the community wherein he has so long labored. A splendid collation prepared by the ladies was partaken of and with cheery social intercourse the hours glided all too swiftly away and brought to a close an occasion that will never be forgotten in the history of the church.

D. M. G.

Carlisle, Pa., April 17, 1899.

HYMN OF JUBILEE

Composed for the Thirtieth Anniversary of
REV. GEORGE NORCROSS, D. D.

BY ELIZABETH L. HALBERT.

(*Tune Webb.*)

Our hearts are glad and joyful
   As on this day we meet,
To offer loving tribute—
   Our pastor dear to greet.
Full thirty years of service
   Have swiftly passed away,
And yet our loving pastor
   Is spared to us to-day.

The growth of tender childhood
   To manhood's riper years,
With joy for all our pleasures,
   With sympathy for tears,
His watchful eye has guarded
   Each step along the way;
And we with loving tribute
   Do honor him to-day.

Young men and maidens also,
   Unite in cheerful strain,
Together with the aged
   Re-echo it again;

Friends far and near assemble
　To celebrate the day,
Which marks a golden mile-stone
　Along the heavenly way.

Thro' sunny days and cloudy,
　Dear Pastor, you have come,
Thro' paths both smooth and rugged,
　You bravely traveled on.
The thirty years have vanished
　Like other years before;
We pray that God may spare you
　For many, many more.

A TRIBUTE

TO REV. GEORGE NORCROSS, D. D.,

On the Occasion of His Thirtieth Anniversary as Pastor of the Second Presbyterian Church.

BY J. WARREN HARPER.

As one, some mountain height to gain,
　Stops, wearied by his rugged way,
And looks far out upon the misty plain,
　Whence he had started at the break of day,

And resting thus, perchance to break his fast,
　While round him falls the mellow set of sun,
Adown the vale his wandering eye is cast,
　Then up and on, ere yet the day be done;

So we to-night upon life's quiet steep,
　While joyous acclimations smite our ears,
Stop for awhile, our festal here to keep,
　And backward look across the stretch of years.

Across the stretch of years, when thou did'st stand,
  Our strong young leader with thy brow aglow,
And we, a remnant now, of goodlier band,
  Thou led'st forth from out the long ago.

When thou, full armored, stood, son of thy Lord,
  Among thy people, so to guard and bless,
Within thy hand the Spirit's two-edged sword,
  Upon thy breast the plate of righteousness.

And so we started forth along life's road,
  Some light of heart and some with bleeding feet
    and torn,
Thy word to cheer as heavier grew the load—
  Life's path no smoothness knows save where by
    duty worn.

If any, fainting, by the wayside fell,
  No pen shall write, no tongue shall ever say,
Thou led'st not thy trusting people well,
  Nor pointed where the danger pit-falls lay.

And when, with bleeding hearts, we mourned our
    dead,
  And lips to brazen heavens dumbly prayed,
So, then, with ours, thy mingling tears were shed,
  On us thy quiet, gentle touch was laid.

Where other leaders smoother pathways sought,
  On fairer plains where bloom'd the lust of pride,
Thou walk'dst the "narrow road" our fathers
    taught,
  Strong in their simple faith, nor turn'd aside.

When lesser minds assail'd thy Church's faith
  And thunders shook its portals; in their track,
Thy ringing battle cry was hurl'd, "Thus saith
  The Lord thy God!" it thundered back.

A TRIBUTE.

And so above the tumult and the brawl,
    Above Dissension's voice, one voice we heard,
Thine own! sharp as the bugle's clarion call
        The simple preaching of the Word.

For thee no beacon on some lesser hill,
    No false torch on the shadow'd meads,
"On! On! Straight On!" thy watch-word still,
    For thee no shifting lights of later creeds.

Beyond, the calm and quiet mountains lay,
    High on their clear-cut peaks God's altars burned,
Straight as the eagle flies, thou kep'st thy way,
    With steadfast gaze press'd on, nor turned.

Lead on! Time hath not touch'd thy sword
    With tell-tale rust, though furrow'd be thy brow;
Lead on! Strong arm of the strong Lord,
    And as we loved thee then, we love thee now.

Beyond and up, with thee we turn our eyes,
    Beyond lie higher steeps as yet untrod,
Beyond! the dawn of Canaan waits! Our Paradise!
    Beyond! the quiet stars, and home, and God!
        Lead on! Lead on!

Hartford, Conn.

CORRESPONDENCE.

A large number of letters full of regrets and congratulations were received. The Committee on Publication regret that they cannot all be printed, but they have been compelled to make a selection. This was a very difficult task, and as they look over the letters which remain unpublished they observe many they would gladly have given to the public. These letters will all be preserved and cherished by the pastor and his family, to whom they are peculiarly sweet and precious.

The first in the series is from Rev. Dr. Radcliffe. Moderator of the General Assembly in the U. S. A., and the honored pastor of the New York Avenue Church, Washington, D. C.:

WASHINGTON, D. C., December 29, 1898.
MR. A. G. MILLER, Chairman Anniversary Services.
  Carlisle, Pa. :

My Dear Brother:—It would give me special pleasure to accept the invitation to the anniversary services of the thirty years' pastorate of my friend and brother, Rev. George Norcross, D. D., but imperative duties here will prevent. I am glad that you are giving public expression to such an interesting and significant event. In these days of short and restless pastorates, it is a compliment, both to the pastor and to the congregation, when they work and live and love together for more than one generation. Dr. Norcross has stood in his place against many a solicitation, and no doubt many a temptation. He has built himself personally into the life and history of all your noble region. Long after his pastorate has ceased, he will speak in the regenerated lives and institutions of your community with vivid and increasing effectiveness. I congratulate you both. The day will be beautiful and bright with many a joyous memory and many an inspiring hope.   Cordially yours,

WALLACE RADCLIFFE.

The following letter is from Rev. Dr. Wm. Henry Roberts, the Stated Clerk of the General Assembly in the United States of America. It was with his personal encouragement that the "Centennial Memorial" was undertaken in 1886, and he pronounced that History the most "unique and complete work" of the kind in the whole Church.

PHILADELPHIA, December 22, 1898.

MR. A. G. MILLER, Chairman.

Dear Sir:—Your kind invitation to attend the Anniversary services in connection with the celebration of the thirty years' pastorate of the Rev. George Norcross, D. D., is cordially acknowledged. I regret, however, that other engagements will prevent my being present on the happy occasion. Allow me to tender to the congregation through you, hearty congratulations upon the auspicious event. The Second Presbyterian Church of Carlisle, Pa., has had in Dr. Norcross a pastor of high qualifications for the care of souls under the great Shepherd of the sheep. A gentleman, a scholar, an admirable preacher, he has united with these qualities that friendliness of manner and that true sympathy which gives a minister of Jesus Christ to be in some measure, "a workman not needing to be ashamed." While however, rendering admirable service in and to the Second Church of Carlisle, Dr. Norcross has also been an efficient Presbyter, and in the wider lines of Church work in Synod and in General Assembly, has been faithful and successful in many things. He is one of the pastors whose influence is as wide as the Church, and whose life, under God's blesssing has been instrumental for good in many directions.

With best wishes for the prosperity of the church in all the future, and for the further growth in usefulness and influence of its beloved pastor, I am,

Yours in Christ,

WM. HENRY ROBERTS.

Rev. Dr. Samuel J. Niccolls, formerly pastor of the Falling Spring Church, Chambersburg, Pa., and now for more than thirty years pastor of the Second Presbyterian Church, St. Louis, Mo., needs no introduction to the Church at large:

ST. LOUIS, December 27, 1898.

My Dear Dr. Norcross:—I have received an invitation to attend the thirtieth anniversary of your pastorate. I wish it were possible for me to be present on that happy occasion. Having passed through a like experience some years ago, I can sympathize with you in the joy of the occasion, and in all of the hopes it inspires. I rejoice that you have been spared so long to the Church, and that you have stood so well the severe test which a thirty years' pastorate in one place brings to a minister. Inertia or obstinacy may keep a man a long time in a pastorate, but to remain for thirty years in a place, holding the affection and esteem of the people, and all the while to be growing in usefulness and power, furnishes an evidence that the pastor has not been negligent in his duty, and that God has been with him. You have not only grown in the affection of your people, but in influence and power throughout the Church. I would fain join with others in bringing to you on your anniversary my testimony of affectionate regard. May the coming years of your service, whether they be long or short, be as bright and as full of happiness and usefulness as the past,

With best wishes, I am,
Fraternally yours,
SAMUEL J. NICCOLLS.

The two following letters are from old classmates at Princeton Theological Seminary. Dr. Wines has been at the head of State Charities in Illinois for many years:

SPRINGFIELD, ILL., December 19, 1898.

My Dear Norcross:—I am glad to be so pleasantly reminded of you once more, by the kind invitation sent me to attend the anniversary services to be observed in connection with the celebration of your thirty years' pastorate on next New Year's day and the Monday following. I wish very much that it were in my power to attend. There is no man in the class to which we both belonged in the theological seminary at Princeton, whom I remember with more respect or affection, although circumstances have prevented our meeting during all these years. I hope that you may live to serve your present charge twenty years more, and then to celebrate your golden wedding as pastor. I am,

Sincerely and cordially your friend and brother,

FRED. H. WINES.

BLAIRSTOWN, N. J., December 26, 1898.

Dear Bro. Norcross:—I was much pleased to be invited to participate in the festivities and congratulations connected with your thirtieth anniversary. We have seen each other so seldom, during these later years, that it was very pleasant to be remembered. For I have always been drawn to you and count you one of my congenial friends. To have kept a large congregation together without friction or dissatisfaction for so long a time is a rare experience, in these days, and shows a rare man. I venture to say that it were easier to do it in the Cumberland Valley than in many other regions: yet, even there, it reveals ability, grace and perseverance.

Please accept my regrets that I cannot be present, and my heartiest wishes for highest usefulness in the remaining and riper years of your ministry.

Your sincere friend,
HENRY S. BUTLER.

The three letters which follow are all from Theological Professors. Dr. Robinson is so well known in this region as to need no introduction. Dr. Beecher has been a professor all his public life. Dr. Lowrie was one of the successors of Dr. Norcross at Galesburg, Ill., and later accepted a professorship in the new Theological Seminary at Omaha:

WESTERN THEOLOGICAL SEMINARY,
ALLEGHENY, PA., December 22, 1898.

Dear Dr Norcross:—With my most sincere regrets that I shall not be able to be present at the thirtieth anniversary of your pastorate over the Second Church of Carlisle, I wish to send my brotherly and very hearty congratulations that you have reached so happy and honorable an occasion. It speaks very definitely and very positively of the ties that have bound you and the people of the Second Church together, of the harmony of spirit and aim that has governed you, of the will of God that has directed your ways. What a tender history do those thirty years contain of personal and family and church life! What gracious dealings of God with you all, what touching memories of commingled sorrows and joys, of common burdens borne for "the name's sake," of new lives started and of saintly lives ended, amid tokens of coming glory!

One cannot but wish he had apprehended the beauty and glory of the ministry of the Gospel when he began it as when its holy opportunities are nearly gone.

I will not write you congratulations on your own fidelity, for the day is dawning on me when I shall be so glad to cast all that I have done at the Saviour's feet, and find my vision filled by Him alone.

Yet I do rejoice in your pastorate at Carlisle. I rejoice that your dear wife has been permitted to share it all with you.

Mrs. Robinson joins in Christian love to you both and to your family.

Yours most sincerely,
T. H. ROBINSON.

THEOLOGICAL SEMINARY,
AUBURN, N. Y., December 29, 1898.

My Dear Dr. Norcross:—I appreciate the honor of being invited to the service in connection with the thirtieth anniversary of your pastorate. It would give me pleasure if I could attend. As I cannot, I send my warmest greetings. I assure you, my dear brother, that our acquaintance, begun before your present pastorate began, has served to deepen the feelings of esteem and love which I have always cherished for you.

Sincerely yours,
WILLIS J. BEECHER.

THEOLOGICAL SEMINARY,
OMAHA, December 28, 1898.

My Dear Dr. Norcross:—I am gratified to receive the invitation to attend the anniversary services to be held in celebration of your thirty years' pastorate. I would be very much pleased if I might be present on so memorable an occasion, but as that is impossible, I must be content with sending you my most hearty congratulations upon a record so notable in these changeful days. I remember when your tenth anniversary came around, good Mother Jackson expressing to me her surprise that you had then been there so long, and had broken what seemed to be the prevailing rule in the length of modern pastorates,—and here it is thirty years! That makes a big slice out of a man's life, if I may be allowed such an expression. We are not as young as we once were; we are better off, not worse, isn't it so?

> Grow old along with me!
> The best is yet to be,
> The last of life, for which the first was made;
> Our times are in His hand
> Who saith, "A whole I planned,
> Youth shows but half; trust God; see all, nor be afraid!"

But, of course, no one can call you old yet, and I trust you may have many more years of usefulness and happiness in the work of the ministry.

With best regards, in which Mrs. Lowrie joins, to yourself and wife, I remain,

Very truly your friend,

MATTHEW B. LOWRIE.

A THIRTIETH ANNIVERSARY.

Rev. Henry Niles, D. D., has been the honored pastor of the First Presbyterian Church, York, Pa., since 1865. He is a man greatly beloved by all who know him. His good wishes follow:

YORK, PA., December 29, 1898.

Dear Bro. Norcross:—Across the intervening distance I extend you my hearty felicitations on this your thirtieth anniversary. However hard to realize the fact, you and I are reckoned among the "fathers" —I trust not fossils!—of the ministry in this part of the country, and on that account, perhaps, I have special right to salute you.

You have been richly blest at Carlisle. With the manifested favor of the Great Head of the Church, and the confidence and loving co-operation of an intelligent, earnest-hearted and affectionate people, yours has been a very successful pastorate.

I should love to join with the multitude who, on Monday, will greet you and yours in person; but circumstances seem to forbid the hope of doing so, and I must be content with saying again—Congratulations and all good wishes!

Yours fraternally,
H. E. NILES.

The following letter is from Rev. Dr. Dixon, Assistant Secretary of the Board of Home Missions. New York city:

156 Fifth Avenue, New York,

December 22, 1898.

My Dear Dr. Norcross:—First of all permit me to offer my heartiest congratulations upon your thirty years' pastorate in the 2nd Church of Carlisle. I am sure that as the years of time and the ages of eternity roll on you will be more and more convinced that there was a nobility and a blessedness in thirty years' pastorate at Carlisle, which will fill your heart with an abiding thankfulness. May the coming days and years bring you increased favor with God and with His people.

I am much pleased with the appeal which you have sent out to the pastors and sessions of the Presbytery. I am sure that it will bring forth fruit and I trust to such an extent as will fill up the measure of our expectation with regard to your Presbytery.

With kindest regards and sincere respect,

I am, Fraternally Yours,

John Dixon.

A THIRTIETH ANNIVERSARY.

The following responses are from two beloved pastors in the Synod of Pennsylvania:

PITTSBURG, PA., December 28, 1898.

My Dear Dr. Norcross:—I have received the kind invitation from the committee having in charge the anniversary services celebrating the thirty years of your pastorate. It would give me great pleasure to be present if it were possible, and I think that so long a term of distinguished service is worthy of celebration. I send you my heartiest congratulations, and desire to express my good wishes for your continued usefulness, and the blessing of God upon you and your Church.

Yours sincerely,
WILLIAM L. McEWAN,
Pastor Third Church, Pittsburg.

—

THE MANSE, FIRST PRESBYTERIAN CHURCH,
MOUNT CARMEL, PA. December 19, 1898.

MR. A. G. MILLER, Chairman:

Dear Sir:—Please accept for the congregation, and convey to Bro. Norcross, my regret that the way does not seem clear for me to attend your services of January 1st and 2nd. I should be glad by my presence to add my congratulations to both Pastor and people upon the testimony that a thirty years' pastorate has given to the world of their faithfulness to each other and to the cause of Christ. May the Lord continue to bless his servant and people with peace, to multiply their seed sown, and to increase the fruits of their righteousness. My family join in congratulations and good wishes.

Yours truly,
STUART MITCHELL.

Dr. Jeffers is always able to speak for himself. We only regret that we could not have had his fun and wit at the anniversary services. His letter will be appreciated by all:

YORK, PA., January 2, 1899.

A. G. MILLER, ESQ., Carlisle, Pa.:

My Dear Mr. Miller:—I thank you and your congregation for the invitation to the anniversary services of your esteemed pastor, Dr. Norcross. If it had been possible, I should have been there yesterday, or would go to-day, to give my personal congratulations to my friend and class-mate on his successful completion of a thirty years' pastorate.

Such things are rare enough to be celebrated when they occur, and good enough to deserve all the congratulations that friends of pastor and people can give. Both parties to a thirty years' co-partnership deserve credit. It bespeaks, excellence, patience and piety in both people and pastor when they work together in harmony for a score and a half of years. So I should like to congratulate pew and pulpit on this happy anniversary. I'm sorry I cannot be there to compare the veteran Presbyter with his student self of thirty-five years ago. He is not so sprightly as he was when I knew him in Princeton, but how much handsomer he is—due, no doubt, to long association with fine-looking people in his home and parish. Then I should enjoy telling how he startled Dr. Green with his grasp of Hebrew, and how, in reciting to Dr. Moffat, the Professor of Church History, he had difficulty in restraining himself from telling more than had been given in the lecture—the historical genius even then giving promise of the valuable contribution he has since made to the history of his denomination. It would be interesting also to recall his perfect familiarity with the whole subject of Pastoral Theology—due, evidently, to the predestined fact that the pupil was to exercise his gifts in the same town where the Professor, Dr. McGill, had delivered his Addisonian sentences in the little Seceder church, that has since seceded to something else. Many other reminiscences come to me when I recall the early days, but I cannot be there to tell them, and this hasty note must convey all my good wishes and greetings. But I cannot close without putting my whole heart into a hope and a prayer that the good work done in Carlisle by my good brother may continue while life and strength are his; and that not one of his faithful words may fall unblest or unfruitful.

Very cordially,

E. T. JEFFERS.

Rev. Robert Mackenzie, D. D., has for many years held the most important post of our denomination in San Francisco. He has declined repeated invitations to city churches in the East:

FIRST PRESBYTERIAN CHURCH,
SAN FRANCISCO, CAL., December 29, 1898.
DR. NORCROSS:

Dear Brother:—Permit me to add my echo to the congratulations that sound about you these New Year days. Long pastorates are so rare in these days, unhappily, that we who follow in the path you have made are fain to salute you.

You are the richest man in Pennsylvania. The accumulations of friendships you have laid up in these thirty years are with you and waiting you. Neither moth nor rust can corrode them. The Cumberland Valley is parent of a goodly host who have wandered far, even to these distant shores, but the dye of its principles defies the washing of years and distance and alien circumstances. It is much to have added your quota to a generation of such stalwart men and sensible women.

I wish you a happy New Year and many of them with a people who love you.

Fraternally,
ROBT. MACKENZIE.

—

The strong personal attachment of Dr. Reigart for the pastor and people of the Second Church must be his apology for the warm commendations expressed in the following letter:

SALISBURY, MD., December 27, 1898.
A. G. MILLER, ESQ., Chairman:

My Dear Sir:—It is a sore disappointment to me that, owing to my pastoral duties, I shall be unable to accept your kind invitation to help to celebrate the thirtieth anniversary of Dr. Norcross' settlement in the Second Presbyterian Church of Carlisle. Having been for over a score of years one of the Doctor's nearest neighbors—in the ministry—and for thirty years one of his best friends, I should like to tell "what I know about the pastor and people of the Second Church of Carlisle." Everybody who knows anything about the people of the Second Church knows—as I do—that they are not, like the Galatians of old, fickle-minded, easily turned aside from the faith, nor like the Athenians, keen in the pursuit of "new things," nor like the people of whom Paul warns Timothy, "who will not endure sound doctrine, but having itching ears heap to themselves teachers after their own lusts," but rather like the Christians of the Apostolic Church who "continued steadfastly in the Apostles teaching," putting in practice and illustrating the precept of Paul to the Corinthians: "Be ye stedfast, unmovable, always abounding in the work of the Lord." Like the phalanx invented by Philip of Macedon, which no enemy could penetrate, the Second Church of Carlisle has presented an unbroken front to the assaults of the rationalism and ritualism of the times. In these restless, changeful days, a thirty years' pastorate is a remarkable thing, and is a strong testimony to the stable character of the people, and their attachment to the truth—for if the truth had not been faithfully preached to the people. this pastoral relation would have been dissolved long ago. It is not because sensational topics have been introduced into the pulpit, or sensational methods adopted in Church worship or work, that Dr. Norcross has held his pulpit so long, but because he has preached the truth—the truth as it is in Jesus—and his people have appreciated that truth.

The people of the Second Church of Carlisle have been well trained and well fed. "Strong meat" has been given them, and they have been able to digest it. Few congregations are the equals of the Second Church in intelligence and education, and no pulpit has excelled in scholarship. The people of the Second Church did a wise thing in putting a pastor's library in the Manse, and then putting a student and scholar in the study. And this student has put his books into his head, and his head into his sermons, and his sermons into the hearts of his people, and this explains the stability and durability of this pastorate. It is the minister who studies who holds his pulpit in these days when "many run to and fro, and knowledge is increased." No people who are "edified" by what they hear from the pulpit will be very desirous of a change. Dr. Norcross has never catered to the prejudices of men. He has never trailed the blue banner of Presbyterianism in the dust. He has done a noble work, not only in the advocacy and defense of the doctrines of Calvinism, but in the honoring of her heroes and exponents. When the detraction of Calvin and Calvinism is so common and popular, he does the cause of truth a noble service who vindicates the character of the men who have held to the truth, and suffered persecution in its defense.

Much is made in these days of "evangelistic" work, as it is called. Its importance cannot be overestimated, unless it is made the sole function of the ministry. But it must not be forgotten, that the training of Christians is as important as the bringing of men into the Church. A minister is a pastor and teacher, as well as an evangelist; and it is because the pastor of the Second Church has taught his people that he has continued so long "in one stay."

But the ministry needed by the Church must not

only be an "educated" ministry, but a spiritual-minded ministry, a sympathetic ministry. Brains without heart have little power. Dr. Norcross is a man of large heart, as well as large head. He is a man of warm sympathies, able to enter into the experiences of joy and sorrow of his people, and therefore he has been able to win their hearts and to hold them.

Dr. Norcross is a most genial companion, a most entertaining talker. His visits to my home when I lived in the Cumberland Valley (and these were frequent, for no two pastors in the Presbytery, I suppose, exchanged pulpits oftener, or assisted each other oftener,) were greatly enjoyed by every member of my family; and my visits to his home were always occasions of great pleasure and profit to myself, whilst there was no church in which I preached with more satisfaction than the Second; and one of my great regrets in leaving the Cumberland Valley was that it took me from the fellowship and society of the pastor and people of the Second Presbyterian Church of Carlisle. The loss of this companionship I greatly feel.

Singularly suited to each other have been the pastor and people of the Second Church, so that it is hard to tell which was the more fortunate, Dr. Norcross in being called to so congenial a field, or the Church in securing so able and worthy a pastor.

Of the results of a pastorate of thirty years no estimate can be made; eternity alone will show its fruit. The record is one of which any man may be justly proud. The blessings of the Head of the Church have rested upon the union entered into thirty years ago, and this is properly made a season of thanksgiving to God, and of gratulation by all the friends of this important Church.

Adding my heartiest congratulations to those of the many who shall take part in this auspicious occasion, I would also join my most earnest prayers for the long continuance of the relation so firmly cemented between pastor and people, eagerly desiring and hoping that the pastor of the Second Church may stand many years to come in his lot, doing the Master's work, and adding jewels to His crown.

Yours very truly,

S. W. REIGART.

Rev. James A. O'Connor, the accomplished editor of the "*Converted Catholic,*" is doing a noble work in New York City in furnishing a home and counsel to priests of the Roman Church, who are sick of her false pretensions. We are glad to print his hearty congratulations:

Christ's Mission, New York,
December 31, 1898.

Rev. Geo. Norcross, D. D., Carlisle, Pa.:

My Dear Doctor:—It would give me great pleasure to be able to accept your cordial invitation to the celebration of your thirty years' pastorate in Carlisle; but as I cannot be present in body, believe me, my spirit, breathing good-will, love, success, prosperity, and many more anniversaries, even to the fiftieth, will be with you.

What good you have done! I know you will say that you have not done half the good you wished. But I believe you will hear by and by the blessed Master saying, " Well done, thou good and faithful servant!" The only title to which a preacher should aspire is to be "a good minister of Jesus Christ," and that should be his eulogy. I think it applies to you, and so thinking, I say so without reserve. With all my heart I rejoice with you and your people, and pray that this New Year may be the best of all for you all.

Affectionately yours,
James A. O'Connor.

Rev. John C. Bliss, D. D., began his ministry in the Second Presbyterian Church. He is now the beloved pastor of the Washington Heights Church, New York city. He writes:

NEW YORK, December 28, 1898.

Dear Mr. Miller:—Accept my thanks for your invitation, on behalf of the congregation, to attend the services next Sabbath, in celebration of the thirty years' pastorate of the Rev. Dr. Norcross.

Most gladly would I be present and a participant on this occasion, did not my duties here prevent.

It seems scarcely possible—indeed, almost dream-like—that so many years have gone since I bade adieu to the Second Church, as the predecessor of Dr. Norcross. How many and how great are the changes which have occurred in this period of time! I suppose that if I could look into the faces of those gathered in the church next Sabbath, there would be but few familiar to me. Inquiring for one and another whom I used to see before me in the old church, it would be told me, "They are no more," and trying to recognize those who remain, who were then children and youth, I should have a difficult task on hand.

There is, however, this blessed consideration, that

whatever changes have been wrought during these years, there has been no change in the word of truth which has continued to be preached to you, nor in the spirit of Christian living engendered by that ministry of the unfailing Gospel.

When I preached my parting sermon to you, over thirty-one years ago, it was from precious words, which now may be well recalled—those in II. Cor. xiii. 11—"Finally, brethren, farewell. Be perfect, be of good comfort, be of one mind, live in peace; and the God of love and peace shall be with you."

I rejoice to know that these divine injunctions have been so fully and so beautifully carried out among you, and that thus the presence and blessing of God have been so manifestly with you.

May His richest benediction rest upon pastor and people in the days and years to come, and may the Second Church abound more and more in the love and service of Him who loved us and gave Himself for us!

Yours affectionately,
JOHN C. BLISS.

The two following letters are from men who have done good service both east and west. The first is a veteran in years and a hero in spirit; the second is a man of brilliant gifts and unflagging industry. He is pastor now of the largest church in Kansas City, Mo.:

FLORENCE, ARIZONA, December 26, 1898.

My Dear Bro. Norcross:—An invitation has been received to attend the anniversary services of your thirty years' pastorate. This little Home Missionary extends his "Briarean arms" of congratulation nearly across the continent. Happy pastor! Blessed people, who have enjoyed his precious services for three decades! What memories cluster around such an event! How many marriage altars! How many funeral sermons performed with rich and balmy consolation! How many souls won to Christ! One generation passed and another coming on the stage! How many baptized children and children's children! How many have crossed the flood, and wait to greet those who

—"A little longer wait,
But how little none can know."

Yes, my dear brother, I bless God that He has spared you to your dear people so many years, and may He spare you another, and if possible two more decades, and you continue to bless and be blessed. God give thee many more souls as a reward of faithful toil, and crown thy labors with abundant success.

For all thou didst for me in the dark days of beginning labors on this hard field, to lighten my labors and bring light out of darkness, and for all that thy people gave may the Lord reward both!

Again I say, God bless thee and thy rejoicing flock on this sweet anniversary occasion.

Very fraternally thine,

I. T. WHITTEMORE.

PHILADELPHIA, PA., January 4, 1899.

Dear Dr. Norcross:—My hearty congratulations on your anniversary! You have had a delightful and successful pastorate, and the Master has given you here great reward. May you continue long in your work and may each year be to you a crown of glory. Wishing you for 1899 a happy year,

Sincerely and fraternally,

H. G. MENDENHALL.

www.ingramcontent.com/pod-product-compliance
Lightning Source LLC
Chambersburg PA
CBHW031941230426
43672CB00010B/2003